MY TIME WITH THE KINGS

AP

MY TIME WITH THE KINGS

A Reporter's Recollections of Martin, Coretta and the Civil Rights Movement

KATHRYN JOHNSON

Introduction by
ANDREW YOUNG

RosettaBooks®
NEW YORK 2016

My Time with the Kings: A Reporter's Recollections of Martin, Coretta and the Civil Rights Movement

First edition published 2016 by RosettaBooks
One Exchange Plaza, Suite 2002,
55 Broadway, New York, NY 10006
www.RosettaBooks.com

ISBN-13: 978-0-7953-4801-3
Library of Congress Control Number: 2015953403

Cover design by Corina Lupp
Interior design by Jay McNair

All archival material courtesy of
Associated Press Corporate Archives, New York, NY

Cover photograph, top: Coretta Scott King and Kathryn Johnson on the campus of Atlanta University in Atlanta, Ga., reviewing plans for The King Center, 1968. *Bottom:* Dr. Martin Luther King Jr. shakes his fist during a speech in Selma, Ala., Feb. 12, 1965. (AP Photo/Horace Cort)

Frontispiece photograph: Dr. Martin Luther King Jr. and his wife, Coretta Scott King, sit with three of their four children in their Atlanta, Ga., home on March 17, 1963. From left are: Martin Luther King III, 5, Dexter Scott, 2, and Yolanda Denise, 7. (AP Photo)

"Let Kathryn in."

—*Coretta Scott King to police officer at door of the King household shortly after her husband's assassination*

CONTENTS

FOREWORD

WHEN KATHRYN JOHNSON WALKED into The Associated Press Atlanta bureau in 1947 looking for a reporting job, there were no women and "they weren't welcome," she recalled. She took a job as a secretary in the bureau with a possibility of someday becoming a journalist. She waited 12 years.

Johnson's reporting career moved faster. She was assigned to the burgeoning civil rights movement because she was "young, green and cheap labor," she said, and because the many white men of the times wanted nothing to do with covering sit-ins, marches and tense black-and-white standoffs.

Johnson rose to become one of the news agency's pre-eminent reporters on the American civil rights era. A deep understanding of Southern culture and people helped her grasp and give voice to the historical transformation taking place. A determined and gracious style got her unprecedented access to the major figures of the time, notably the family of Dr. Martin Luther King Jr. In her nearly 20 years of reporting for AP, she would break some of the most important stories. Beyond civil rights, she covered the My Lai massacre hearings and the court-martial of Lt. William Calley, the travails of the wives of American POWs in

Hanoi and their eventual release and readjustment to civilian life.

There was a fearlessness about her when on assignment. She was petite, only 5 feet 3 inches, but never "too worried about some of the very dangerous situations that took place." She had an ability to look the part, dressing as a coed to sneak into class alongside Charlayne Hunter when she integrated the University of Georgia in 1961.

Born in 1926 in Columbus, Georgia, to John Lewis and Lula Boondry Johnson, she grew up in a strictly segregated world. "Everything was black and white," she said. "It never occurred to me that this was wrong, segregation."

She described her childhood as part "Huckleberry Finn," trailing an older brother and his friends sometimes into trouble and at other moments into danger. She was rescued from drowning by two elderly African-American fishermen as a small boat she was floating in sank in the Chattahoochee River. Later the boys shot a tin can off her head with a .22-caliber rifle as she replaced the can after each shot. "Fortunately, they were excellent shots," she said.

Throughout her career, Kathryn encountered the "standard" treatment of women of the era and bureau life. One day she would be taking dictation and compiling high school sports scores. On another she would be in the street covering what likely was the top story in the nation.

When she found herself still assigned to dictation and sports scores even after completing a Nieman Fellowship at Harvard, she decided to leave the AP. She worked for U.S. News and World Report in Washington and later for CNN in Atlanta.

But her heart remained with AP and its mission. She fell in love with writing and reporting at a young age. She embraced the front lines of journalism and its eyewitness role to history. She—like many of the people she covered—tasted discrimination firsthand. Kathryn Johnson never turned bitter. She embodied journalism's highest ideals—that the work we do ultimately makes the world better, fairer and safer. In so doing, she inspired generations of AP colleagues, both male and female.

Tom Curley
Former AP president and CEO

INTRODUCTION

FOR MORE THAN 10 years, I had known Kathryn Johnson as she covered the civil rights movement and the historic change that swept the South.

Kathryn always observed scrupulously the highest standards of her profession while reporting on one of the most important continuing struggles in our country with objectivity, thoroughness and fairness. Like many other reporters, she sometimes faced personal danger in order to fulfill those duties.

Whenever anything was happening, Kathryn seemed to be there.

She has written of being trapped in an outside phone booth by several Ku Klux Klansmen when a Freedom Bus was arriving; locked in a deli in downtown Atlanta along with students trying to integrate; and forced to sit in a hot courtroom gallery while covering the trial of two Klansmen for the random killing of a black Army Reserve officer, Lt. Col. Lemuel Penn.

I remember when Coretta Scott King spoke of Kathryn's remarkable tenacity—in that she alone, of all those involved in the racial conflict, covered the King family for three generations. Starting with Martin Luther King Jr. on his return to Atlanta after heading the fight in Montgomery, Alabama, to integrate city buses, she persistently followed King and the Movement through the whole of his tumultuous career.

And that, along with friendship with Coretta after years of interviewing her, is why Coretta allowed Kathryn, alone of all the journalists covering civil rights, to be present in the King home on the night her husband was assassinated and every subsequent day until his burial.

Of all the significant stories Kathryn reported, those of the civil rights movement mean the most to her. Moreover, her reporting on racial conflicts, murder trials, assassinations and protests managed to secure access for AP photographers, resulting in exclusive, historic photos that may have been impossible to obtain otherwise.

In Kathryn I have observed such qualities as boundless curiosity, impressive character, humility and fidelity to her work. Such thorough, accurate, courageous and firsthand reporting is sometimes slow, and by the standards of today's social media generation, may seem old-fashioned. But of such stuff is a great reporter made.

And that is a precise description of Kathryn Johnson.

Andrew Young

PREFACE

As a white girl born and reared in the Deep South, I grew up in a rigidly segregated society. I always thought, "That's the way it is." I'd barely begun as a full-fledged Associated Press reporter when that thought was quickly transformed by the civil rights struggle that was spreading rapidly across the South in the 1960s.

I first began covering Dr. Martin Luther King Jr. in 1960 at news conferences, sit-ins and demonstrations, when he was a young, fairly unknown Baptist minister. But it wasn't until he ended a strike near downtown Atlanta and I offered him a ride home that I began to really know King and his wife, Coretta, personally.

I'd written features for the state wire about Coretta and how she had given up a promising singing career to marry King and about the difficulties of caring for four children while her husband was often out of town. Occasionally, Coretta invited me to have lunch with her and I would often visit for a chat. I'll always remember our time together.

The '60s were powerful days. Blacks were taking to the streets while America was pouring more and more of its blood and money into the Vietnam War. To say I was unprepared for plunging into chaotic events is an understatement. I had not the slightest idea of what I'd be facing. Yet, in the first few years, I was trapped and rattled in an outside phone booth by Ku Klux Klansmen; held at gunpoint by an Alabama state trooper and a taxi driver; hit by rocks and tear gas in race riots; locked in an Atlanta deli with sit-in demonstrators; and forced to sit in a scorching-hot courtroom gallery while covering the trial of two Klansmen for killing Lemuel Penn, a black Army officer.

Of all the trials I reported, none has haunted me as much as the 1964 Lemuel Penn murder trial in Danielsville, Georgia. When I heard the words "not guilty" from the all-white jury, I wasn't really surprised, knowing how blacks in the Deep South were treated at that time. How could they not convict the two Klansmen with such overwhelming evidence against them? Yet no way were they going to convict white men for the random killing of a black. That trial taught me how cruel and unjust the South's judicial system was for black citizens, who were routinely called Negroes or colored people back then.

This is my account of those years, which I spent reporting for The Associated Press during the height of the civil rights movement.

Kathryn Johnson
Atlanta, Ga.
2015

1

'LET KATHRYN IN'

IT WAS RAINING HARD in Atlanta on the night King was assassinated. I was on a date with a friend, heading to a movie, when the bulletin broke in on the car radio.

At first, neither of us spoke. Then my date asked, "Want me to drive you to the King home?" I nodded. He turned the car around and drove straight there, both of us silent, stunned and locked in our own thoughts.

At the King home, now on Sunset Street, I made a dash in the spring rain for the small porch of the modest, split-level redbrick home with its barred windows. The dark, tree-lined street was ablaze with lights. On the porch, I recognized a New York Times reporter talking to a policeman, who told us no reporters were allowed in the house.

As we stood there, the door opened to let someone out. Down the long hall, I could see Coretta, clad in a rose-pink nightgown and robe. Spotting me, she told the officer, "Let Kathryn in."

Visitors, including King's sister, Christine, and her husband, Isaac Farris, and many close friends, had been filling the King home. After most had left, Coretta, needing rest and privacy, went into seclusion. She gestured for her eldest daughter, Yolanda (known in the family as Yoki), and me to join her in her bedroom. The younger children had gone to bed.

Coretta, recovering from surgery she'd had weeks earlier, lay back on the pillows of her large bed, watching television. Reports were flowing in about her husband's death, with reruns of dramatic moments in his life.

The three of us were mesmerized before the TV screen, watching King's face and listening to the powerful and prophetic last speech he had made only the night before in Memphis, Tennessee. As his voice thundered, "I am not afraid. ...Blessed is the name of the Lord," Coretta wept softly.

On that night, rain had been falling in Memphis, too. Lightning flashes shone through the windows of the Masonic Temple, where King was speaking to a crowd of some 2,000, many of them members of the striking garbage workers' union he had come to support.

"I just want to do God's will," King said, his rhythmic words punctuated by thunder crashing outside and picked up by the microphone. "And he's allowed me to go up to the mountaintop, and I've looked over and I've seen the promised land." His words and his somber thoughts seemed to stir the crowd. "I may not get there with you. But I want you to know tonight that we as a people will get to the promised land!"

While Coretta, Yoki and I were watching those dramatic events, the phone rang. I heard Coretta say, "Mr. President." I assumed Lyndon Johnson was on the line to express condolences, and I left the room briefly to give her privacy.

After she hung up, Coretta called me and we went back to watching TV. She did not say anything about her phone conversation, to me or to her daughter, nor did we ask. Tight-lipped and misty-eyed, she began again listening intently to what her husband was saying, but her face was calm.

I've no idea what Coretta was thinking that night, though I've often been asked. If I had to guess, it would be about her devastating loss, about how she and her four children were going to get along, or perhaps how she could carry on her husband's remarkable legacy. King was 39 years old.

That night, April 4, 1968, Coretta displayed the same resolute will and remarkable composure that would carry her through the kaleidoscopic events and emotions surrounding her husband's assassination and burial.

A young photographer for the Southern Christian Leadership Conference (SCLC), who had been told to record the happenings in the King home, came into the bedroom briefly and began snapping pictures. Twelve-year-old Yoki, in pajamas and robe and her hair in pink curlers, lay on her stomach on the floor, her face propped between her hands.

Not wanting to intrude in pictures of Coretta at such a poignant time, I left my chair and flopped down on the floor next to Yoki, stretching to one side so that I could stay out of view of the camera.

When the photographer finished, I got back in my chair. It was eerie. The famed civil rights leader and Nobel Peace Prize winner had just been shot to death and there we were, his wife, child and I, watching in awed silence as he spoke: "We've got some difficult days ahead, but it really doesn't matter with me now, because I've been to the mountaintop."

Listening to that emotional, intellectually charged voice was stunning, realizing that never again would we hear live the sound of his voice and the power of his words. I felt a strong sense of unreality being in the King home at the end of his life, since I had been there covering many events early in his rise to fame.

I was also feeling a strong sense of privilege for being in the King family's home during that difficult time.

On his last night, King's thoughts seemed riveted on death. There had been threats, he told his Memphis audience. Only that morning, bomb threats had delayed his commercial airliner for a baggage search in Atlanta.

Days after his death, Coretta had said, "We always knew this could happen." Only weeks before, King had sent her a bouquet of plastic flowers. "Why plastic?" Coretta had asked. "You've always sent me real flowers."

King replied, "They're to remember me by."

2

VISITING KING'S HOME

ON A FIERCELY COLD winter night in 1964, I was trudging alongside Dr. Martin Luther King Jr. as he led a group of striking marchers at Scripto, a pen and pencil–manufacturing plant near downtown Atlanta.

Bundled in a heavy coat, my teeth chattering from the cold, I asked King the usual questions: "How much pay raise are they asking? Where are negotiations at this point? Do you plan to continue striking?"

Scripto workers had walked off the job, demanding equal pay with whites for skilled and nonskilled work. King sympathized with the strikers, many of whom were members of his church.

The straggly little group hurrying along the cold, dark city street drew little media attention except from one or two local TV reporters.

By sheer luck, that assignment led to my meeting later in the privacy of the King home and to my personal introduction to his incredible gifts as an orator.

King, ending the freezing march at 11:15 p.m., told me, "This is a dangerous section of town. Let me escort you to your car." When we reached my car several blocks away, I offered to drive him home. At that time, the Kings lived on nearby Johnson Street.

As I stopped the car to let King out, his wife, Coretta, pregnant with their last child, came to the door and said, "Come on in and have some hot coffee. You'll warm up." King led me to a phone in his office, and I quickly called in my strike story.

I then joined the couple at their dining room table, sipping coffee and talking about what had become known as the Movement. I'd long been impressed with King's personal magnetism and flow of words at news conferences, but sitting at their table late that night, I was struck by his simple brilliance as a leader.

His ability to put into words the longings, the hopes and dreams of his people, their anguish and their cry for human dignity, clearly was a great gift.

After that night—although King was known for never calling reporters by their first names—he always called me Kathryn.

King was to me a young, well-educated Baptist minister who came out of the Jim Crow churches of the South preaching brotherhood and nonviolence. But it was into a land filled with violence. Blacks were being beaten, lynched and terrorized by Ku Klux Klansmen who drove into their neighborhoods wearing their long white robes and hooded masks to frighten them. King, too, had been threatened—a bomb had been thrown at his home in Montgomery, Alabama, and later in

Atlanta, Klan night riders had burned a cross in his front yard.

It was 1:15 a.m. before I left the King home, and both King and Coretta stood at the door waiting until I drove off.

At home that morning, I took a breakfast tray into the den so that I could watch TV news. When the Scripto strike story came on, my mother, spotting me as the only white person in the crowd and walking alongside King, questioning him, said, “Honey, be careful. I’m afraid someday someone’s going to try to kill that man.”

3

GRIEF AND TRUST

DURING THE FIVE HARROWING days that followed the assassination, Coretta stayed busy answering phone calls and dealing with nagging, solemn decisions: what services to have and where, who was to speak, what hymns to sing and who was to sing them.

She had meetings with her sister-in-law, Christine Farris; her husband's top aide, Andrew Young; his secretary, Dora McDonald; and friends, the Rev. Ralph Abernathy, Hosea Williams, Jesse Jackson and many others. Some meetings were held in the King home, others at Ebenezer Church, the SCLC office and elsewhere.

Watching Coretta discuss plans with civil rights leaders, I realized she was missing privacy in her mourning. Not only were varied decisions being thrust at her, but she had to deal with the tears of her four children.

Listening to the now fatherless children question their mother filled me with sadness. "Who's going to be my daddy now?" asked 5-year-old Bernice. Coretta told her, "Uncle Ralph, Uncle Andy," referring to the Rev. Abernathy and Andy Young.

Yoki had taken her younger brother, 7-year-old Dexter, on her lap and spoke about their father. "I'm not going to cry, I know Daddy's gone to heaven," she said, tears streaming down her face. "Maybe someday I'll meet him there."

While funeral plans were discussed privately in the back, in King's study, I sat on the floor in the living room, daily crowded with visitors. It was a memento-filled room, with a camel seat from Egypt and a painting titled "Integration" by the great-great-granddaughter of John Brown, the 19th-century abolitionist.

On a small lamp table were an ivory carving and small bust of Mohandas Gandhi, who led the successful struggle for India's independence from Britain. King had often said that Gandhi had inspired him to apply the same principles of nonviolence in the movement for equal rights.

Coretta, tied up with visitors and decision making, one afternoon asked if I'd drive her husband's father, universally known as Daddy King, to the stadium to watch the Atlanta Braves practice. Her father-in-law loved baseball and Coretta told me she wanted him to have some diversion.

A stocky, gray-haired man who had a sometimes bawdy but always a delightful sense of humor, Daddy King was inconsolable over the death of his eldest son and muttered only "hello" to me.

Since none of the family was to be home for a while,

Coretta asked if I'd take Dexter along for the ride. On our drive to the stadium, Daddy King, clad in a dark gray suit, was so morose that I made a comment or two about the Braves players, but my efforts were futile. Wrapped in grief, he barely answered.

Apparently someone had phoned Braves officials that Daddy King was coming, since he was met by several officials when I dropped him off at the ballpark. Then I headed home to pick up a jacket before driving Dexter home. As we rode along Ponce de Leon Avenue, the child, missing his grandfather and family, started crying.

Stopping for a red light, I noticed a police car next to me, both officers staring at the little black boy sitting next to me, tears flowing down his face. This was not something you often saw in Atlanta in 1968—a white woman with a crying black child. Would they stop me? If they inquired and found out I had Martin Luther King's child, would they think I'd kidnapped him?

Quickly, I decided to drive to a friend's home a few blocks away. Helen Mackris Burleigh wasn't home, but her mother was. She gave Dexter a hug and asked, "How would you like cookies and a Coke?" Dexter, holding cookies in one hand and a Coke in the other, was soon smiling and playing with kittens in the backyard.

Coretta continued to consult daily with civil rights and church leaders over funeral plans. She decided services would be held at Ebenezer Baptist, the church where King, and his father and maternal grandfather before him, had preached the doctrines of human dignity.

The old redbrick church on a corner of Auburn Avenue, founded in 1886, had been a touchstone for King throughout his turbulent career. It was at Ebenezer that the young King grew up and there that he returned as co-pastor with his father after his role as a civil rights leader brought him international fame.

One night after a day of long meetings, Coretta came home about 11 p.m., kicked off her shoes and sat wearily down on a sofa to chat with a small group of friends and relatives. We told her that a white couple who had driven all the way from Boston for the funeral was in another room, waiting to meet her. "These people have been here for hours," Coretta said, putting her shoes back on and going, gracious and composed, to talk with the couple.

When funeral plans were finally agreed on, it was decided that Dr. Benjamin Mays, the highly respected president emeritus of Morehouse College and King's friend, teacher and mentor, would lead the services.

Now that I knew plans were final, I asked Coretta if it was OK for me to phone my office, and she said yes—an agreement that incidentally gave AP an 11-hour beat over archrival UP.

With all the pressures Coretta faced, I felt I was somewhat under pressure, too. I had to check daily with her to make certain that the plans I was phoning in were final and accurate before dictating to my office. Such rare access gave AP a tremendous inside-the-home advantage over other media.

The AP never divulged that I was the sole reporter in the house for five days, nor did that come out in our stories. But my fellow reporters gathered on the King lawn outside knew. Some were already there when I arrived early from my home.

Every day, friends of the Kings, white and black, filled the home. They helped out by answering phones, preparing meals for the family and visitors, cleaning the house, or simply sorting through the thousands of telegrams that poured in from throughout the world.

Telegrams were stacked on the dining room table and on smaller tables in other rooms, and I pitched in to help the young girls who had volunteered to sort and catalog them. As we sifted through the huge pile of mail, we occasionally had to dodge the two young King boys, running around the rooms.

As I read telegrams and letters by the hour, I was struck by how people from all walks of life had written, from heads of state to those who had followed King as a messiah. A woman in New York said only, "I am a nobody, but I'm sorry." I used her quote in one of my stories.

4

THE FINAL FIGHT

THE EVENTS THAT LED up to King's death had begun on a cold, gray February morning in Memphis. Rain had fallen but barely enough to send trickles of water along the streets and sidewalks.

The city's sanitation department sent home 22 street cleaners, all blacks, with only two hours' pay. They complained that white supervisors got a full day's pay, even when it rained.

Complaints swelled into a strike of more than a thousand garbage collectors and resulted in clashes with police and hundreds of arrests.

And it brought King, whose nonviolent creed was under ever-deepening challenge from young Black Power advocates, to Memphis, where he led the sanitation workers in marches.

Just a week before King was killed, a crowd of black teenage militants had turned a march into a window-smashing rampage, with looting and fighting with police.

To King, their outbreak was a repudiation of all he'd been preaching. Never one to give up, he planned to lead a massive march down the path where violence had broken out to again demonstrate that peaceful ways would prevail in the struggle for civil rights.

The day that he was shot, a court order in Memphis banned any additional marches, and King agreed to delay the proposed march from the next day, a Friday, until Monday.

King's trusted aide, Andy Young, asked U.S. District Judge Bailey Brown to withdraw the order. The judge asked Young what effect withholding the upcoming march would have on King.

"I would say that Dr. King would consider it a repudiation of his philosophy and his whole way of life," Young replied. "I don't know when I've seen him as discouraged and depressed."

Shortly after 3 o'clock Thursday afternoon, a neatly dressed white man arrived at a cheap rooming house a block west of the black-owned Lorraine Motel in Memphis.

He gave his name as John Willard and told the manager he only wanted a room to sleep in. He was led upstairs to Room No. 5, looked it over and said, "This will be fine," then paid a week's rent: $8.50.

The window in a bathroom located down the hall opened on a seedy lot, and at a certain angle, an occupant could see the section of the Lorraine Motel where King was staying. King liked the Lorraine, and especially the catfish steak, a house specialty.

On April 4, he was standing on the balcony, chatting with several friends as they prepared to leave for a rally scheduled for that night. Suddenly, a rifle shot rang out, slamming King backward, his smile turned into a dazed look as he crumpled to the concrete floor.

At the hospital, hope slipped away. King died in the emergency room at 7 p.m. of a gunshot wound in the neck. Charlie Kelly, the AP photographer in Memphis for the marches, had gone to the hospital. Kelly told me that Andy Young had come to the door to notify the waiting news media. His face tear streaked, he pointed to his throat, to show where King was fatally shot, and whispered softly, "He's dead."

5

KING'S BODY COMES HOME

THE NEXT MORNING, I was sitting in the King living room when I heard Coretta say that she wanted to fly to Memphis to bring her husband's body home. Sen. Robert Kennedy of New York, who was taking an increased interest in civil rights, had offered his private plane for the one-day flight.

At the Atlanta airport before Coretta boarded, Yolanda asked her, "Should I hate the man who killed Daddy?"

Coretta told her, "No, you shouldn't. It's not the Christian way."

Coretta was accompanied on the plane by Christine Farris, Dora McDonald, Andy Young's wife Jean, and a few other friends.

Reporters, photographers, leaders of the civil rights movement and others were waiting for Coretta's entourage to board. On the spur of the moment, I asked, "Andy, can you squeeze me in on the flight?"

He turned to several aides standing nearby and after a quick check, turned toward me and said, "Yes."

This prompted howls from other reporters,

particularly television newsmen. Andy held a hand up, stopping them with a decisive, "Kathryn and I've been through the wars together."

I began rapidly rummaging through my large handbag for a dime to call my bureau chief but couldn't find one. Standing next to me was Jesse Jackson, then the northern director of SCLC's Operation Breadbasket in Chicago.

"Jesse," I said, "I don't have a dime on me, and I need to call my office, can I borrow one?" He rolled his eyes upward as if to say, "A reporter without a dime!" He dug in his pocket and handed me the coin.

I phoned my boss, positively elated that I'd fly to Memphis with the small group so in the spotlight. Unfortunately, our bureau chief was not elated, and told me, "No, we need you in the bureau at this time." I've no doubt that had I been male, my boss would have been delighted for me to go. After all, the King assassination was a world story and a reporter with Coretta would have enhanced our coverage.

While in Memphis, Coretta went to the funeral home to view her husband's body. Later, back home, she told me she had not liked the suit that had been put on him and ordered it changed.

The plane returned that night and I was among the hundreds of people waiting at the airport when it landed. The crowd surged around, and Coretta stood briefly in the open doorway above the stairs.

Clad in black, her eyes swollen, she paused to greet her four young children, who had waited several hours under somber skies and a slight drizzle. They ran up into the arms of their mother. She and her children stood in the doorway as her husband's bronze casket was rolled down a ramp and into a waiting hearse. From there, it was taken to a funeral home on Auburn Avenue.

Several days later, Coretta flew back to Memphis with her three oldest children to lead a march that her husband had planned in support of the garbage workers' strike. Thousands followed her through the city, and Coretta told the marchers, "This is what he wanted"—to continue his fight.

6

THE VIEWING

After a few days, the body of Dr. King was brought to Spelman College, one of America's oldest historically black schools for women, for public viewing. It was laid in the Sisters Chapel on the campus. The hearse was to arrive at 4 p.m. but was more than an hour and a half late.

While waiting for the chapel doors to open, mourners stood outside beneath a great elm; others sat on newspapers along the urns or on the stone steps between the chapel's large white columns. They waited quietly, without complaint.

Finally, the doors of the chapel opened and long lines filed slowly past King's bier, peering sorrowfully through the glass at his face.

Students filed by, and children, men and women, some well dressed, others in work clothes. Many wept, their hands to their eyes as they sobbed softly in the often unbridled emotion of black people of the South.

In the gathering darkness as the evening wore on, more whites appeared to pay last respects, including clergymen and nuns who had marched nonviolently for voting rights with King at Selma in 1965.

On the night that Coretta took her children to view their father's body, neither she nor her children wept or touched the bronze coffin. They stood close together, gazing in silence, as Daddy King rocked back and forth over the casket, screaming, sobbing and trying to claw away the glass that separated him from his dead son.

The long line of mourners waited in deferential silence until Daddy King finally collapsed and was led away by several men. His display of grief was, for me, one of the most heart-wrenching moments of that day.

Thousands of visitors streamed into Atlanta by air, buses, private jets and cars, turning King's hometown into a center of mourning. They stood in line endlessly on Spelman's green spring campus, with its lacy dogwoods in bloom, to view his body: the famous—Sidney Poitier, Bill Cosby, Paul Newman, Sammy Davis Jr., Eartha Kitt—and the unknown. The college area was tied up with cars, their headlights on in token of mourning.

Meanwhile, my office was checking reports that King's killer had fled Memphis in a white Mustang and that such a car had been spotted in Atlanta. Several of us were sent out on a fruitless search in the downtown area for the car.

On June 8, 1968, James Earl Ray was arrested, and nine months later, he confessed to killing King.

Nonetheless, rumors swirled about a conspiracy. How could a man such as Ray, a common burglar and armed robber, have managed to get a false identity, a passport, and fly to England, where he was captured? Could he really have done it alone? Those questions have never been answered.

7

ON THE INSIDE, IN THE KITCHEN

On the day of King's funeral, April 9, 1968, I awoke at dawn to a pink sky, the rising sun burning off mist and splashing over azaleas and pink and white dogwood trees in full bloom.

The early spring beauty seemed a strange backdrop for the solemn tone of the day, the coming burial services and the havoc that we had been warned might occur in Atlanta. In the five days since King's assassination, violence had shaken more than a dozen U.S. cities.

I'd left home to drive to the bureau to write a story about the expected arrival of former First Lady Jacqueline Kennedy. I left instructions that my story was to be held until I could verify that she had actually visited the King home. A colleague drove me to their home so I wouldn't have to deal with my car.

I needed to be inside the King house early, since the Secret Service would be extremely busy handling large crowds. Every day, Coretta had to inform the agents that I could be there. But on the morning of the funeral, with the entire world focused on the tragic and historic event, I thought asking her again to vouch for my presence would be graceless.

So I made myself part of the King household. I went into the kitchen, took off the jacket of my dark blue suit, tied on an apron I found hanging nearby and rummaged through the kitchen cabinets, pulling out several large frying pans. I began cooking bacon and eggs for the Kings' four children and Coretta's mother and father.

Earlier that morning, Coretta had risen to greet her parents, Mr. and Mrs. Obadiah Scott, who had driven from their farm in Marion County, Alabama. The couple brought with them a dressed pig, which they stored in a freezer, then sat down at the kitchen table.

They spoke very little while I cooked. Coretta's father, a kindly faced, gray-haired man, suggested his toast was a bit overdone. It was. I was trying to hurry everyone through breakfast so I wouldn't miss the arrival of Jackie Kennedy. I quickly retoasted some bread for Mr. Scott, with an eye always turned toward the living room.

Meanwhile, Bernice, the Kings' bright-eyed 5-year-old, who was called Bunny, spilled orange juice on the skirt of her crisp white dress. I hastily washed the stained spot off the skirt and ironed it so she could be dressed in time.

Needless to say, as I was busy fixing breakfast, I was never questioned by the Secret Service and I even offered hot coffee to the agents guarding the back of the house.

A white volunteer secretary of Coretta's was in a back room, King's office, answering a constantly ringing phone. The guests, mostly women clad in black mourning clothes, sat quietly in a circle of chairs in the living room, while Coretta remained secluded.

The doorbell rang. Jackie Kennedy and her friend Rachel Mellon had arrived from Washington. While someone was telling Coretta that her famous guest—whom Coretta had personally invited—was there, I stood at the entrance to the dining room, still wearing an apron and holding a dish towel.

Mrs. Kennedy, glancing around the living room full of mourners, spotted me. Before greeting anyone, she made a beeline toward me and, to my great astonishment, shook my hand. I can only guess that since I was obviously clad for the kitchen, she assumed I was the Kings' white maid.

By then, Coretta had come to greet her guests and the two widows clasped hands, Mrs. Kennedy whispering words of comfort. Both women, wearing similar black silk suits, moved slowly down the long hall to the bedroom, where they spent five minutes in private conversation.

Afterward, Mrs. Kennedy and Mrs. Mellon left for the church in a limousine. As soon as they were out the door, I picked up a phone to call the AP office.

I wanted them to release my already written story since Mrs. Kennedy had made her condolence visit. Also, I needed to update the story briefly but found myself being watched intently by several guests who knew I was a reporter. I was concerned that a few resented my presence in the King home.

Since my conversation was within earshot of guests and I was enduring some hard stares, I said to the staffer who answered, "Hello, Mother, this is Kathryn. I just want to let you know that Mrs. Kennedy has been to the King home and is now leaving for the church."

It was a signal, meaning: "Mrs. Kennedy has been here, put my already written story on the wires." However, the staffer who answered had not been in the office when I had gone by at dawn.

"Lady, you have the wrong number," he said, sending my heart into a fast beat for fear he was about to hang up on me.

Summoning up as much calm as I could muster, I said, "Noooo... this is Kathryn."

"Oh, is this Kathryn?" he asked. "Are you trying to tell me something?"

"Yessss."

Finally, my message got through and my story moved.

Coretta and her entourage took off for Ebenezer while I, family members and guests were driven in separate cars. We were soon slowed by the thousands of people jamming the streets surrounding the church.

8

RITES FOR A DRUM MAJOR

King's murder touched off a cataclysmic rampage of violence that shook the nation. Neighborhoods in more than a dozen cities erupted in outrage, with the worst burning and plundering in Chicago and the nation's capital.

Thousands of soldiers poured into Washington to protect the White House and the fire-scarred national capital. Fires and looting scourged several black neighborhoods, and trails of smoke hung in the spring sky. A soldier manned a machine gun on the steps of the Capitol, giving it the air of a banana republic. Before the fury was spent, some 100 cities and towns were hit by fires or looting or both. The Department of Justice counted 46 dead, all but five of them black. I thought how ironic the violence was in the aftermath of the assassination of a man often called "the apostle of nonviolence."

In Atlanta that day, there was no such madness. City and state officials had worried that King's death and the magnitude of the crowds would cause an emotional backlash and ordered National Guardsmen into the Atlanta area. Our office, too, warned us of possible violence and offered gas masks to reporters covering the story.

But King's hometown was peaceful, dignified and respectful. Despite worries about what might happen, it was obvious to those of us covering the funeral that Atlantans, more sorrowful than angry, aimed to honor King as he had lived his life—peacefully.

Mourners had dressed their small children in their Sunday best, taking them along to join or watch the gathering crowds around the church. No way, I thought, would they have brought young children along, had they expected violence.

People poured in from across an anguished nation—airlines, charter flights, buses and private cars brought in thousands. Crowds gathered early outside Ebenezer, watching the invitation-only guests go inside. Mrs. King was accompanied by singer and civil rights activist Harry Belafonte.

Cheers greeted the arrival of entertainers, sports personalities and other notables, including Vice President Hubert Humphrey, representing President Lyndon Johnson; Jacqueline Kennedy; Sen. Robert Kennedy and his wife, Ethel; Gov. Nelson Rockefeller of New York; Sen. Eugene McCarthy of Minnesota; former Vice President Richard Nixon (who would be elected president that November); Gov. George Romney of Michigan; former Gov. Carl Sanders of Georgia and

Black Power advocate Stokely Carmichael. Looming above all were the head and shoulders of 7-foot-tall basketball star Wilt Chamberlain.

By the time services began, tens of thousands of people lined Auburn Avenue all the way to downtown Peachtree Street, determined to pay final respects to the leader who had forged for them a powerful new weapon, nonviolent protest.

Crowds were so dense that it was almost impossible for anyone to move. Amid the jostling and yelling, you could hear an outburst of an occasional temper flare.

"Man, you gotta move," an officer told one man just outside the church. "You can't stand here."

"Man, I just moved. They said I couldn't stand there."

"You gotta move."

"Where to?"

"You gotta move. We gotta clear the way."

The AP had worked out a plan for reporters. As one left the church to phone in to writers from New York and Washington, now in the Atlanta office putting together major stories about the daylong outpouring of tributes, another staffer would go into the church to pick up the coverage.

In the pew where Coretta sat, her youngest child, Bunny, was in her lap chewing her fingernails. Bunny finally fell asleep against Coretta, who lifted her black veil, revealing a face etched in grief.

Tears were running down Andy Young's face as he sat on the podium while Dr. Benjamin Mays delivered his eulogy.

Tall, solemn, gray-haired Dr. Mays told the congregation: "How strange. God called the grandson of a slave... and said to him, 'Martin Luther, speak to America.'"

Mostly I remember the voices of two soloists. Mahalia Jackson's low crooning kept up with the superb voice of Mary Gurley in measured, mournful tones as Gurley, a young member of Ebenezer's choir, sang "My Heavenly Father Watches Over Me." It was a duet of great beauty.

Gurley's low sad notes from "My Precious Lord" shook the congregation with their soulfulness, and the congregation responded with sobs and shouts: "Oh, yes," "Yessir" and "Jesus."

Soon it was my turn to observe America's notables coming out of the church. In order to gain a vantage point over the crowds flowing down Auburn Avenue like a river, I climbed on top of the King hearse.

In front of the hearse was the rickety old wooden farm cart drawn by two Georgia mules, a symbol of King's championing of the poor. They were ready to escort King's body through the city in a march unlike any he'd ever been in.

Suddenly, I heard King's loud voice in a familiar sermon, "Drum Major Instinct," the last sermon King had given at Ebenezer. Coretta had asked that his recorded voice be piped outside as it was being played in the church and it dramatically keynoted the quiet, dignified funeral service.

King's voice rang out: "Every now and then, I think about my own death, and I think about my own funeral. I don't want a long funeral. Tell them not to mention that I have a Nobel Peace Prize—that isn't important. If you want to, say that I was a drum major, say that I was a drum major for justice...."

I caught myself listening to that rich, vibrant voice, the voice that was called "the great instrument of the civil rights movement." King's thundering words piped loudly from the church and echoed down Auburn Avenue.

Those words were well-known over the world, but they rushed over me with a special shock of recognition. They brought back to me a day just two months earlier when I heard them for the first time directly from King's lips.

I'd taped them on Feb. 4 at Ebenezer, after King's secretary, Dora McDonald, had phoned me. Dora had a reputation for trying to keep reporters away from King, who was always pressured for time. But that same efficient, protective secretary was now requesting that I turn up on Sunday. She had already phoned our top civil rights reporter, Don McKee, but he was tied up with other work.

Dora would only tell me that the sermon would be "important." I wanted to hear it, but I was also due for a rare Sunday off, since weekend desk work was often a grueling regular shift for me. I phoned our bureau chief to ask him to get someone to cover it, but he told me AP's budget was strapped and he could not authorize overtime.

Our Atlanta budget was always blown—news events were breaking so fast in the South that reporters had to be sent out hastily in every direction. I also knew my boss realized that if I considered a story worthy enough, I'd cover it on my own time.

Fearful that I might miss something important, I went to Ebenezer that Sunday, copying King's words on my notepad as fast as I could as he delivered his now famous "Drum Major Instinct" sermon. I also taped it in its entirety, hurried back to the office, wrote a quick story for AP radio (which commanded fast-breaking deadlines), then typed a lengthy story for Monday morning newspapers.

Since I felt I had that sermon exclusively—at least, I'd seen no other reporters in the church—I stayed on to write the story for the next day's afternoon dailies, working some 12 hours altogether. Both stories quickly went out on AP's top wires.

Now, two months later, I was sitting on top of King's hearse, hearing that same sermon in King's oratorical voice, ringing out in his own eulogy. That familiar voice rumbled through the church and outside to the tens of thousands of people jamming Atlanta streets on that beautiful spring day.

"Yes, if you want to say that I was a drum major, say that I was a drum major for justice. Say that I was a drum major for peace; I was a drum major for righteousness. And all of the other shallow things will not matter."

Listening again to the sermon, punctuated by the rich emotionalism of taped response from the congregation, made me appreciative that AP had preserved this moment so that the world could hear that thundering call for equality at this very moment.

Ebenezer always recorded Sunday sermons and so did the SCLC, but the difference was that AP had the ability to send it worldwide and it had quickly become well-known. I began then to realize that what I'd been covering all those years made a difference.

9

THE LAST MARCH

THE VAST THRONG OUTSIDE Ebenezer finally grew so restive that police ordered the funeral march to begin early, even before the private church service ended. And tens of thousands, caught up in the power of a massive and overwhelming bereavement, began to walk, some crying, others singing.

Thousands more stayed behind to await the body. A little after noon, church bells tolled again at Ebenezer and I, still on top of the hearse, watched as the family emerged from the church, followed by the coffin and visitors.

I was rapidly jotting down names of the senators, governors, civil rights leaders, ambassadors of many of the world's countries, show business celebrities, prominent preachers and rabbis. Emperor Haile Selassie of Ethiopia in a long black cloak and Archbishop Iakovos, head of the Greek Orthodox Church of North and South America, with his flowing black silk robe and the tall miter on his head trailing a long black veil, were commanding figures.

Several men hitched King's bronze casket onto the faded green farm wagon and the 4-mile procession to the cemetery began. In life, King was always at the head of the marches. On this day, though, his body, resting on the creaking wooden wagon drawn by two decrepit-looking mules, was far back, preceded on its final journey by thousands and followed by tens of thousands.

Those of us who had reported on King in marches through Southern towns were used to seeing him met with white hostility or disdain. But this day in his hometown, whites were also in the march or standing respectfully on sidewalks, as the never-ending crowd of marchers, 30 abreast, surged through downtown streets.

Mostly, though, the procession of marchers was filled with sorrowful black faces. Some wore overalls; others were in their Sunday best. There were nuns in black garb and priests, politicians, entertainers, the curious, the young and old. One marcher was pushing a baby carriage. A few umbrellas were raised against the hot sun, and a few women had discarded their shoes.

Solemn and silent behind the mule-drawn bier, the marchers frequently burst into song: "Freedom, Freedom" and "Before I Be a Slave, I Be Buried in My Grave." And the most haunting of all, "We Shall Overcome," that surging song of hope that built up courage for many on long, hot, dusty protest marches in the South.

As we rounded the Georgia Capitol, we were met with a strange scene. More than 100 helmeted state troopers, armed with shotguns and other weapons, stared out of drawn curtains as the massive funeral procession passed peacefully around the Capitol. The sight of the troopers did not discourage the marchers.

Georgia's segregationist governor, Lester Maddox, refusing to attend the funeral, was holed up in the Capitol surrounded by state troopers.

Earlier, Maddox was furious when he saw that the state and national flags had been lowered to half-staff the day after King was shot, in his honor. Maddox called Georgia Secretary of State Ben Fortson, demanding that the flags be raised. Fortson told him the flags had been lowered by order of President Johnson. They stayed lowered.

As the marchers again started singing "We Shall Overcome," I thought of how King, a symbol to the marchers of all their hopes for a better life, had made it possible for them to believe that they could—and would—see a change in America. When they reached City Hall, they stopped briefly and sang "The Battle Hymn of the Republic."

A church bell tolled mournfully as they passed the Catholic Shrine of the Immaculate Conception, an old redbrick church spared by Gen. William Tecumseh Sherman when he burned Atlanta more than a century earlier.

Under a broiling Georgia sun, the river of humanity followed the mule-drawn wagon as it crept to Morehouse College, King's alma mater. There, outdoor services were held on the green quadrangle, rimmed with blooming dogwood trees.

After that, the mourners marched with King for the last time, following his wreath-shrouded coffin lying on the old farm wagon. In uneven lines, they trailed it the rest of the 4 miles to the red clay soil in South View Cemetery. The graveyard was founded in 1866, right after the Civil War, by blacks who, tired of taking their dead to the back gates of public cemeteries, wanted to bury them with dignity.

I was lucky to hitch a ride from Morehouse to the cemetery, where the daylong rites drew to an end on a grassy slope. Interment rites were brief. "Earth to earth, ashes to ashes and dust to dust," came the familiar ritual from the Rev. Abernathy. "We give thanks to God who gave us a peaceful warrior who was willing to die but not willing to kill."

King's grief-stricken father placed his head on his slain son's coffin and wept. Coretta, dry-eyed throughout the ritual, wept silently.

Emperor Haile Selassie, a bearded, diminutive but regal figure, placed a wreath on King's tomb. Then he leaned down and spoke softly to King's mother, affectionately known to all as Mama King. She did not speak but simply bowed her head and nodded.

The long day ended as King's casket was placed in a tomb of Georgia marble. Engraved on it were the closing words from an old slave song that King had used in his moving speech during his Washington March in 1963: "Free at last, free at last. Thank God Almighty, I'm free at last."

A photographer from England, Harry Benson, had climbed up onto a high crypt just above the heads of the King family. Perched there, he shot pictures of King's coffin as it was being placed in the crypt. AP photographer Charlie Kelly told me that in that high spot, Benson seemed so much an authority figure that when another photographer tried to climb up, Benson yelled at police below, in his British accent: "Don't let him up."

A police officer then told the man, "He says you can't come up there."

AP photographer Charlie Tasnadi had brought a 12-foot ladder with him and after sitting awhile on it, decided the mourners were slow in arriving, so he left to join them. He told a man sitting nearby, "Don't let anyone on my ladder."

When Tasnadi came back, a very large black man was sitting on top of his ladder. "Sir, that's my ladder," the photographer, who happened to be white, told him.

The man didn't move. "Sir, I don't think you understand; this is my ladder."

The man on top replied, "This ladder is under new management."

After King's body was placed in the crypt beside his maternal grandparents, the scene of humanity trampling on flowers and around graves was chaotic enough to belong in a Federico Fellini movie.

By this time, the skies were overcast and rain threatened while mourners swarmed all over a hillside of flowers, snatching them up for souvenirs.

The funeral procession was unique in American history, and no one who took part in it will ever forget it. The sorrowful procession, estimated by police at 150,000, was an overwhelming force in itself and a fitting tribute to the slain leader.

During the long walk back to my office, my biggest concern was the usual one in the '60s—to find a telephone. In that era, cell phones and laptops were nonexistent.

AP staffers covering the funeral needed to phone writers in our office who were waiting anxiously for details. All day, they had been filing one story after the other, updating them as staffers called in. I ducked into a store and pointing to press credentials hanging around my neck, told the manager, "I'm a reporter and need to phone in fast as I can. I won't be long." He nodded and pointed to his phone.

By then, all of a sudden, I felt extremely weary, but there was no way of hitching a ride back downtown. Along with countless thousands, I walked all the way back to the Atlanta newspaper building, which then housed AP.

Finally, I'd finished my five-day assignment. As I walked back into the bureau, into that wire service world of constant pressure, dominated by noise from jangling telephones, dozens of clacking Teletype machines and clouds of cigarette smoke, I felt the need for peace.

Walking down the hall to a sitting room, I flopped into the nearest comfortable chair. Resting there at long last, with no urgent demands facing me, I thought again of hearing King's drum major speech being piped outside Ebenezer.

And it struck me—now that I was free of reacting coolly to events of that fateful week as a dispassionate reporter—that the drum major would march no more.

Reporters, focusing hard on a story, are somehow protected from emotional reactions—at least, they've acquired enough discipline to keep their emotions in check. Now, suddenly, I felt overwhelmed with such sadness and fatigue that it was hours before I could drag myself out of my chair and finally head home.

The following Sunday was Easter and I went back to Ebenezer, again on my own time, for a story. Coretta took the pulpit to tell the congregation that continuing her husband's unfinished work would be the greatest tribute to him.

Daddy King walked slowly to the pulpit and said, "These are mysterious and perilous times in which we live. And many times, our hopes are shattered. But never lose your faith—keep your faith."

"I'm not going to let the devil put me in a corner," he said, his voice rising. "My head is bloodied but unbowed. This is Easter morning. Oh, yes, he's up." A refrain rose from the congregation, "He's up, he's up."

Then, the gray-haired father of a slain son bowed his head and said, "You may have come here frustrated this morning, but the Lord stands ready to help. He's such a good and kind savior. I love him. I love the Lord. As long as I live, I'll love the Lord!"

Abruptly, Daddy King shut his Bible and walked over to the side of the church where his wife, daughter and other relatives sat. "Well, that's all I'm going to say," he told the congregation, his broad shoulders drooping. "I promised my wife I wouldn't overdo."

Coretta Scott King, widow of civil rights leader Martin Luther King Jr., arrives for a memorial service at the American Federation of State, County and Municipal Employees, AFL-CIO convention in Miami Beach, Fla., June 4, 1968. (AP Photo/Jim Bourdier)

King stands on the balcony of the Lorraine Motel in Memphis, Tenn., on April 3, 1968, a day before his assassination at approximately the same place. From left are Hosea Williams, Jesse Jackson, King, and Ralph Abernathy. (AP Photo)

King makes his last public appearance at the Mason Temple in Memphis, Tenn., on April 3, 1968. (AP Photo/Charles Kelly)

Six men hang a sign in honor of slain civil rights leader Dr. Martin Luther King Jr. at an expressway bridge in Atlanta, Ga., April 8, 1968. (AP Photo/ Toby Massey)

Coretta Scott King is shown with her daughter, Bernice, during her husband's funeral at the Ebenezer Baptist Church in Atlanta, Ga., April 9, 1968. (AP Photo)

Coretta Scott King, right, is accompanied by her children Yolanda, Bernice, Martin III, and Dexter at an open casket viewing at Spellman College in Atlanta, Ga., Sunday, April 8, 1968. (AP Photo/Jack Thornell)

A brace of plow mules pulls King's casket along the funeral procession route in Atlanta, Ga., April 9, 1968. Reverend Jesse Jackson and Andrew Young, at the left corner of the casket, are among the mourners. (AP Photo)

Coretta Scott King is comforted in the doorway of an airliner in Memphis, Tenn., April 5, 1968, as her husband's body is brought up the ramp. (AP Photo)

Coretta Scott King relaxes in her bedroom in Atlanta, Ga., on May 28, 1968, as secretary Barbara Hicks opens one of the many packages that arrived through the mail. (AP Photo/Kathryn Johnson)

Kathryn interviewing Martin Luther King Sr., "Daddy King," in his office in Atlanta, Ga., 1968. (Kathryn Johnson Collection)

Coretta Scott King and Kathryn on the campus of Atlanta University in Atlanta, Ga., reviewing plans for The King Center, 1968. (Kathryn Johnson Collection)

Coretta Scott King poses in front of a portrait of her husband in her office in Atlanta, Ga., 1972. (Kathryn Johnson Collection/Joe Halloway Jr.)

10

GROWING UP

MY TWO SIBLINGS AND I were born in Columbus, Georgia, then a quiet Southern town separated from Alabama by the Chattahoochee River—which, to our delight, was just across the street and down a steep bluff. My brother, Lewis, was the oldest; I was next, then my sister, Rita.

Like many Southern children of the day, we felt genuine affection for a few blacks as individuals, but as group, they were nameless and indistinguishable.

The only ones we knew personally were Inez Daniel, our longtime nurse (today called a nanny), and our yardman, John. We children loved Inez, who was hired when we were very young—she was only 15. We cried so much when it was time for her to leave at the end of each day that she had to sneak out the back door.

I often sat on the front porch on summer days, watching black women strolling along our sidewalk, balancing on their scarf-wrapped heads large wicker baskets of fruit and vegetables and singing out, "To-may-toes, straw-ber-rees." Inez would go out to choose what to buy—and argue over prices.

I got a rare inside glimpse of the wretched poverty in which most blacks in the Deep South lived when Mother took me with her to give leftover baby clothes and blankets to Inez's mother, who had 16 children.

I saw the barely furnished three-room shotgun homes (so called because a bullet shot from a gun through the front room would go straight out the back) and the cracked walls, the bare floors, the brutal poverty in which they lived.

All my young life, I'd driven by those shabby, pathetic shanties but it never occurred to me that change could, or should, occur. I was unaware of other barbarities in their lives—lack of education, the right to vote, and most glaring of all, the Jim Crow laws of segregation.

My first glimpse of violent racism occurred when I was 6 years old, riding a city bus with Mother. A policeman boarded, walked straight to the back, grabbed a black man and began beating him with a nightstick.

As blood ran down the man's shirt, I asked, "Mama, why is that policeman beating that man?" Since my voice was easily heard throughout the bus, Mother grabbed my hand and we got off at the very next bus stop, even though it wasn't ours.

Each year, our town celebrated Confederate Memorial Day in a parade that began on a green, tree-lined parkway, near the river. My siblings and I had no Confederate ancestors, yet we celebrated with as much alacrity as our playmates. With bands blaring music, the parade began at a tall granite Confederate memorial obelisk, several blocks up from our home.

My brother's best buddies were the Pennell boys, who lived across the street from the monument in the Bethune Plantation, a 24-room Victorian mansion. The four boys grew up listening to tales handed down from their great-grandparents, who had fought in the Civil War.

One day, while rummaging through an old trunk in their attic, Sam Pennell and my brother discovered a cache of old Confederate money consisting of hundreds of $20 and $50 bills. We played with that money for years.

As children, Lewis, Rita and I were unaware of the South's conflicted past. Most of our ancestors had arrived from Greece in the late 1880s. I learned how pro-Confederacy our hometown was when the Columbus Confederate Naval Museum opened. Its industries had manufactured uniforms, swords, pistols, rifles and small cannon—all for the Confederacy.

11

EARLY REPORTING YEARS

SIT-INS, PROTEST MARCHES AND Freedom Rides came my way, I felt, because I was green, cheap labor and the men with experience didn't want to cover them. At least not until Martin Luther King became famous. My colleagues were traditional Southern men with traditional Southern views.

I'd turned to the American Newspaper Guild to help me become an AP reporter, and the Guild had fought to give me the chance. I had a degree in English literature and had studied journalism for a year at Georgia State. I had to because my college, Agnes Scott, did not have a journalism course.

I was delighted when my chance to try out came, although I knew the Atlanta bureau of The Associated Press wanted no women on its staff. One Atlanta staffer, Don McKee, was assigned exclusively to civil rights, and he covered the subject masterfully. When he was out of town, I was sent to cover a variety of civil rights skirmishes. The struggle for civil rights had filled much of the 1950s but had died down after the successful city bus boycott in Montgomery, Alabama, in 1956, led by Dr. King.

It began accelerating in September 1960 after several black students sat in at a lunch counter in Greensboro, North Carolina, and asked for a cup of coffee. When refused, they sat patiently; when told by police to leave, they left as other activists filled their places. If attacked, the students employed King's nonviolent strategy, curling up into a ball and expecting blows. That strategy gave life to the Movement.

Hoping to find ideas for feature stories, I strolled around the campuses of Atlanta's six black colleges and universities, chatting with students, professors, policemen and anyone else I came across. I called Dr. Benjamin Mays, then president of Morehouse College, who had long been King's mentor, and asked for an interview.

Mays, a quiet, composed man and a profoundly moving speaker, was born in the town of Ninety Six, South Carolina, in 1894, to parents who were freed slaves. I was the interviewer, but I spent that hour learning about early civil rights—or the lack of them—and what life was like for rural blacks in the South at the time.

Another time, while talking with a couple of black policemen in predominantly black Mozeley Park, I realized how little opportunity there was for better-paying jobs. To my surprise, I found that both officers were graduates of Morehouse, one of Atlanta's most prestigious black colleges. Despite their degrees, they were unable to find jobs in their fields.

Atlanta had black doctors, lawyers and businessmen, but in those years they mostly served the black community. Now I was beginning to understand how brutal and dehumanizing segregation was, while getting to know blacks as individuals and equals. It was a transforming experience.

I was sent to get a feature on a gathering of the Links Club, whose members included black professionals, graduates of Atlanta's black colleges and universities. That day, for the very first time, I found myself sipping a soda and chatting casually with interesting and knowledgeable black men and women in a social setting.

At another function, an attractive, beautifully gowned black woman asked if I'd met the wife of a prominent civil rights activist in Washington. Yes, I had. She then asked, "Is she black, light, pecan, caramel... What color?" That was my first knowledge of the interest in the various hues of skin color among black women. I felt saddened, knowing that segregation had brought about this thinking.

12

HOT GRITS

While King's assassination left indelible memories in my mind, other events during that chaotic era have also stuck with me. Most involve young people whose names never became well-known, despite their courage.

When black college students in Atlanta attempted to integrate the downtown Krystal (one in a chain of small fast-food restaurants), I stood in the back, watching. They ordered burgers and Cokes, but instead of delivering their order, white grill men dumped bowls of hot grits on their heads.

Watching the grits drip slowly down onto the shoulders of the young men, who sat enduring the indignity in silent protest, aroused my indignation and sense of justice.

I was inside the same Krystal when its counter was again pre-empted, this time by robed Ku Klux Klansmen. Outside, a group of blacks, primed for a sit-in, lined the sidewalk, alongside police officers.

At this time, the Student Nonviolent Coordinating Committee (popularly called SNCC) had been organized to bypass older groups thought to be too slow in pushing for change.

After the Klansmen had eaten and began leaving, a group of SNCC members surged toward the door, singing, charging and scuffling with police. Thirty-three were arrested, including James Forman, then executive secretary of SNCC. Five blacks went to the police station to protest the arrests, and they, too, were arrested.

At another demonstration, I'd been questioning Forman, a stocky young man who could slip easily into crude, profane language. He needed a typewriter, he told me, and worried he'd have no time to walk to the building that housed the Southern Christian Leadership Conference offices and back, with a demonstration still going on. I was about to leave for my nearby office and suggested he come and use my typewriter.

As he typed away, we both got hard stares from a few of my fellow staffers. Forman had to be aware of the unspoken hostility, but he ignored it, finished typing, gathered his papers, thanked me curtly and left.

From then on, I could usually get Forman, who was difficult to contact, to come to the phone whenever I needed to question him on a story.

13

BELOVED STORE

BLACKS AND WHITES ALIKE loved Rich's, a large department store in downtown Atlanta with a reputation for allowing customers to return purchases—even years later. It was so popular in Atlanta that columnist Celestine Sibley wrote a book about it entitled "Dear Store."

In October of 1960, our office had a call that black students would attempt to integrate the Magnolia Room, an upscale dining room in Rich's. I went to the dining area, sat and ordered lunch. Soon, a group of well-dressed black college students, accompanied by Martin Luther King, quietly walked into the Magnolia Room and began sitting at tables that were empty. All were arrested and charged with violating Georgia's trespassing law.

A few older black waitresses stood silently apart, watching the attempts to integrate. For years, they had been in the Magnolia Room only to serve; now young blacks were demanding seats at a table. A middle-aged black female elevator operator, stepping out to watch, spotted my reporter's ID and said to me, with a big smile, "I'm real glad and real proud!"

After the protesters spent five days in jail, all but King were released. He remained in jail on a technicality that came from his being on probation for a traffic violation.

A month earlier, King had pleaded guilty to a routine charge—driving without a valid Georgia license. With all the chaotic events crashing around King and having recently moved his family to Atlanta from Montgomery, he had forgotten to renew his license on time. He was fined $25 and put on 12 months' probation. The judge treated the Rich's sit-in as a violation of probation and ordered that King be jailed.

He was sentenced to four months' hard labor at Reidsville State Prison, which then had a notorious reputation for brutality. "Oh no!" groaned several staffers in our office upon hearing where King was to be sent. Fearing for his safety, we were afraid more incendiary news would follow.

At this time, the presidential election campaign between Richard Nixon and John Kennedy was a tight contest. Coretta King had phoned a contact in the Kennedy campaign, saying she feared her husband would be killed in prison. Her call was returned by JFK himself, who expressed concern and sympathy.

Then his brother Robert Kennedy phoned to assure Mrs. King that he would do all he could to make sure her husband would be safe. He also called the judge, who determined that King could be released on bail.

Some critics felt the Kennedys' help in freeing King was a political move for the election. King's release affected Southern politics by causing many black voters to switch from the Republican Party—the party of Lincoln that had freed the slaves—and vote Democratic.

King's father, a lifelong Republican, now said publicly he would vote for Kennedy. His son, however, would not tell who would get his vote. Kennedy won a very close election, with heavy black support.

Often, after working a particularly rough day, a few reporters from my office and the Atlanta newspapers would meet at Dante's Down the Hatch, a favorite bar at Underground Atlanta. Dante's featured fondue with drinks, along with a close look at live alligators swimming in a deep, long narrow pool near the bar.

We'd share anecdotes and I told them about a phone call I'd gotten the night before from a Ku Klux Klansman. The call came at 3 a.m. and woke me from a sound sleep. I'd first thought the office must be calling me in again on overtime. Then I heard the voice of a man who gave no name but said he was a Klansman and threatened me because of a bylined story of mine.

I don't recall his exact words, but with more late-night calls from the KKK assailing my stories, it wasn't long before I got an unlisted phone number.

14

FREEDOM RIDERS

As racial turmoil washed over the South in the summer of 1961, Alabama became the focus of Freedom Riders, students who sat in the front seats of Greyhound buses headed south. Their action was bold, courageous—and very dangerous.

Only a year before, the U.S. Supreme Court had declared the segregation of passengers on interstate buses to be unconstitutional, but the ruling was ignored by Southern states.

The idea of Freedom Rides had come from the Congress of Racial Equality (CORE), an interracial, nonviolent group. They began challenging racial barriers by riding in the front seats of buses heading for Mobile, Alabama; New Orleans and Shreveport, Louisiana; or Jackson, Mississippi.

The rides on Greyhound buses full of Freedom Riders were generally uneventful—that is, until the bus reached Alabama. One heading for Birmingham never made it. Its only scheduled stop was Anniston, Alabama, where angry whites threw stones and bricks at the bus and slashed the tires. The bus pulled swiftly away, stopping outside the city, only to be attacked again by a mob. The bus was firebombed, and passengers barely got out before it burst into flames.

When other integrated buses arrived at a transfer point, whites as well as blacks sitting together up front were sometimes brutally beaten or thrown in jail. Too often, enraged racists had time to attack protesters before police or the state patrol arrived.

John Siegenthaler, an aide to U.S. Assistant Attorney General John Doar, was sent to Montgomery to negotiate protection for Freedom Riders, but he was knocked unconscious by an angry mob that met the bus. That spurred the U.S. Justice Department to take action to protect the riders.

In Birmingham, a Greyhound bus trip was canceled by the driver, who stood at the side of his bus and told Freedom Riders attempting to board, "I have only one life to give, and I don't intend to give it for CORE and for the NAACP [National Association for the Advancement of Colored People]."

When I was sent to Montgomery to meet an integrated bus, our AP correspondent there, Rex Thomas, warned, "Be careful!" After watching the Greyhound bus arrive, I began phoning my Atlanta office from an outside phone booth when several angry white men spotted me dictating. They ran over, grabbed the phone booth, yanked it off its moorings and rattled it, with me inside.

AP photographer Horace Cort, spotting my plight from his car, drove close by, threw open his car door and yelled, "Katy! Get in!" The men, startled, quit shaking the booth for a moment, giving me a chance to get off the floor, grab my briefcase, and scramble out and into the car, and off we sped.

Kathryn Johnson during the start of her career at The Associated Press, circa 1957. (Kathryn Johnson Collection)

King is welcomed by his wife, Coretta, after leaving court in Montgomery, Ala., March 22, 1956. King was found guilty of conspiracy to boycott city buses, but a judge suspended his $500 fine pending appeal. (AP Photo/Gene Herrick)

King leaves court after a four-month sentence in Atlanta, Ga., Oct. 25, 1960, for taking part in a lunch counter sit-in at Rich's department store. (AP Photo)

A Freedom Rider bus went up in flames in May 1961 when a fire bomb was tossed through a window near Anniston, Ala. The bus was testing bus station segregation in the south. (AP Photo)

Kathryn (far right) reports on Vivian Malone and James Hood; the two African-American students registered at the University of Alabama at Tuscaloosa, Ala., June 11, 1963. (Kathryn Johnson Collection)

The author, left, donned bobby socks and a sweater to obtain the only eyewitness story of Charlayne Hunter's first day of class at the University of Georgia in Athens, Ga., Jan. 11, 1961. (AP Photo)

Charlayne Hunter, 18, the first black woman to attend University of Georgia, sits in one of her classes in Athens, Ga., on Jan. 11, 1961. (AP Photo)

Charlayne Hunter, accompanied by Dean William Tate, clutches a small Madonna statue with tear-filled eyes as she leaves the University of Georgia campus in a State Patrol car, Jan. 12, 1961. (Kathryn Johnson Collection)

Gov. George Wallace blocks the entrance to the University of Alabama as he turns back a federal officer attempting to enroll two black students at the university campus in Tuscaloosa, Ala., June 11, 1963. (AP Photo)

State troopers swing billy clubs to break up a civil rights voting march in Selma, Ala., March 7, 1965. Future U.S. Congressman John Lewis is being beaten in the foreground; he sustained a fractured skull. (AP Photo)

King waves as marchers cross the Alabama River on the first of a five-day, 50-mile march to the state capitol at Montgomery, Ala., on March 21, 1965. (AP Photo)

Civil rights demonstrators in protest of Rep.-elect Julian Bond being denied a seat in the House because of his statements opposing U.S. participation in Viet Nam, Atlanta, Ga., Jan. 14, 1966 (AP Photo/Horace Cort)

Stokely Carmichael, national head of the Student Nonviolent Coordinating Committee, speaks on the campus of Florida A&M University, April 16, 1967, in Tallahassee, Fla. (AP Photo)

15

NOBEL PEACE PRIZE

DR. KING WAS IN an Atlanta hospital for a routine checkup in 1964 when Coretta phoned to tell him she'd been notified from Oslo, Norway, that he had been awarded the Nobel Prize for Peace.

I hurried to the hospital to get King's reaction as well as comments from hospital aides and nurses who were lining up to hear what he had to say to the small group of reporters and photographers.

Clad in pajamas and robe, King proudly told us his prize was a fitting tribute to the "millions of gallant Negroes and white persons who have followed a non-violent course" in the struggle for equal rights.

He was the third black, the 12th American and the youngest man ever to win the award. King, who never sought wealth and often expressed the opinion that "money corrupts," said he intended to spend every dollar of the prize money—$53,123—on the civil rights movement, with the Southern Christian Leadership Conference, which he headed, getting most of it. That struck me as perhaps misguided, as his four young children had yet to face college.

When the conference ended, reporters and photographers lined up to shake his hand—the first time I had ever seen this happen. King, who rarely smiled—at least in public—was smiling happily and shaking every hand.

One of the first visitors to the hospital to congratulate him was Archbishop Paul Hallinan of the Catholic Diocese in Atlanta. King's secretary told me that Hallinan had privately asked if he could bless King, and did. Then, the archbishop surprised King by asking him for his blessing.

Reaction around the country ranged from "eminently appropriate" from a church leader, to "shame on somebody" from a segregationist.

Controversy always swirled around King; not everyone approved of his tactics or was swayed by his oratory. FBI director J. Edgar Hoover, a longtime personal opponent of King's, at a news conference called King "the most notorious liar in the country."

After he won the prize, Coretta underscored the contrasts in her husband's career when she remarked, "I wish we could remain on this mountaintop forever. For the past 10 years, we have lived with the threat of death always present."

16

LOCKED IN LEB'S

THE MOST UNUSUAL AND fascinating sit-in I ever covered took place at Leb's, a popular New York–style deli in downtown Atlanta, picketed more than any other restaurant in the city.

By 1964, many of Atlanta's restaurants and hotels had agreed to desegregate. Those that refused were being targeted by youths belonging to SNCC.

The deli's owner, Charles Lebedin, often called Leb, shook his bald head at me as I interviewed him, saying bitterly, "Why have the Negroes chosen me for their demonstrations? Why me?"

His restaurant had just been the scene of demonstrations for four days, and when a group of SNCC members came in on a Saturday in January of '64 and waited to be served, I was inside the deli. Leb refused the young protesters service and asked police to evict and arrest them. Police refused. Leb then locked the doors to the entrance and restrooms.

I'd been questioning several demonstrators when I saw Leb locking his large front doors. I walked to the entrance and tried the handle. To no surprise, it wouldn't open.

All of us, protesters and restaurant workers—to my knowledge there were no other reporters—were locked inside for several hours. Since I'd not had time for lunch, I tried to order a sandwich but got nothing but harsh stares from Leb's white waiters.

Despite our weird plight, I was not afraid, since the SNCC youths were not unruly. But I was somewhat appalled when a few who were refused entrance to the locked men's room urinated publicly into the deli's coffeepots. They stood leaning against the counter, their backs mostly to us and holding the coffeepots in their hands, while mouthing off angrily.

After a while, the front door was unlocked and the standoff inside ended. But outside, trouble awaited. A group of Klansmen, headed by Atlanta's Klan chief, Calvin Craig, had begun marching in front of Leb's and around the block.

I knew that Craig's Klan chapter had renounced violence, but the SNCC activists then started their own march, trying to occupy the same stretch of sidewalk with the Klan. Jeering black youths began taunting Klan members, and the noisy opposing marchers started yelling angrily.

I'd intended to make a quick dash to the AP office only a few blocks away to write, but seeing SNCC marchers brush elbows against the Klan, I hung around, convinced that violence would break out. Unbelievably, the two close marches ended with no major incidents.

The next morning, unruly SNCC activists again gathered outside Leb's and tried to charge into the front door, but they were blocked by police.

"Where am I? Am I back in Russia?" Leb asked, his voice loud and emotional, his hands rising in the air. "I'm not a racist. I'm a Jew, and I know what persecution is. I was born in Russia, on the Polish border. When I was 5 years old my family had to flee for their lives after the czar fell. Many members of my family were killed. My father, who was an attorney in Russia, had to work as a laborer in America and my sister, in a factory.

"Why should I gamble on losing everything I've worked all my life to get, by integrating? If every Atlanta restaurant would integrate, I'd be happy to do so. But the ones who say they're integrated are not. They're hypocritical—the Negroes don't bother them—but their business has fallen off. I'm bewildered," he said, shaking his head slowly.

I asked, "What will you do if the public accommodations section of the civil rights bill passes?" The bill was then before Congress.

"If the government passes it, I'll do what the law says," he answered.

For four more days, Leb's was the scene of mass demonstrations by blacks and a few whites. More than 100 kicking, screaming demonstrators were arrested after lying down in the middle of the street in front of the restaurant.

"No one has ever been singled out as I have," Leb told me. "I am very bitter, very hurt. I'm a strong segregationist now. I wasn't always. The Negroes have made me that way with their methods," he said, his eyes slightly red-rimmed from sleepless hours of coping with his problems.

"Why can't I get police protection?" was another recurring question Leb kept asking. "The demonstrators were arrested on the street, but Saturday night, when 260 of them came into my restaurant, I couldn't get police to arrest them." Police had declined to make arrests in places of business unless proprietors signed warrants.

"I asked a police captain where I could get a warrant on a Saturday afternoon," Leb continued. "He told me he didn't know. They have a new city rule now that you have to go to the courthouse, which closes at 3 p.m., and swear out a warrant for each demonstrator in order to get them to leave your property.

"Mobs were jamming my windows. White customers

left and I closed the restaurant at 4 p.m., sent my help home, and still 38 Negroes refused to leave."

The demonstrators damaged restaurant fixtures, said Leb, shaking his head. "I ask you," he added, waving his arms excitedly, "why can't a man close his business when he wants to?"

17

INTEGRATING SOUTHERN UNIVERSITIES

THERE WAS VERY LITTLE school integration in the Deep South, despite the Supreme Court decision of 1954, and integrating the University of Georgia and the University of Alabama loomed as very major stories.

Each university integration was different and I was confronted on both stories—as I often was—without the luxury of planning. Coping with such matters was a major part of the challenge.

On a balmy January morning in 1961, Charlayne Hunter, 18, and Hamilton Holmes, 19, trudged along the oak- and elm-lined walkways at the University of Georgia, about to sweep aside nearly two centuries of segregation.

All reporters—and there were scores of us—were banned from the buildings where the two were about to enter their first classes. Both were escorted by a federal officer, walking quietly along behind them, and they were followed by curious students.

I had already met Charlayne and Hamilton in

Atlanta when I interviewed them before they left for the university.

I was following Charlayne, and we were chatting briefly when several students came over, reached out and shook hands with her. "Nice to have you," they said.

Others paid no attention to the attractive, wistful-eyed young woman who had a ready smile for all. Tagging along behind her, I could detect no feelings of resentment or antagonism from the cluster of students.

I figured reporters would be barred from Charlayne's first class, so while packing my bag for the drive to Athens, I thought of trying to pass myself off as a student. That way I could observe how the class reacted to her. I took clothes that would blend in with what coeds were wearing—bobby socks and saddle oxfords.

When she reached Meigs Hall, which housed her psychology class, she walked up the stairs, where several university officials sat at a desk, screening students. They were preventing news people from getting near her classroom—or so the university thought. The media had been ordered to remain at the bottom of the stairs.

I waited there until I saw Charlayne pause briefly at the officials' desk. When she walked away, I started up the stairs. Glancing down at the photographers clustered at the bottom, I wondered if they would complain to authorities about me. Not one, not even the

UP guy, did, although it was obvious I was trying to sneak in.

Carrying borrowed books, I stopped at the desk. "What class?" an official asked tersely.

"Psychology 101," I answered. He pointed ahead and I walked on into the classroom where Charlayne was seated in an aisle seat. No one sat next to her—most classmates were across the aisle.

I chose a seat several rows behind, so Charlayne wouldn't notice me, but I could observe any reactions by her classmates.

The professor took no roll call, nor did he acknowledge her presence; he just began lecturing. Charlayne sat alone and poised, listening to him explain the history of behavior patterns in psychology while quietly making history herself.

Fashionably dressed in a green sweater with matching blue-green checkered skirt, she scribbled lecture notes in a notebook, as I did. When the bell rang, several girls walked over to her, smiling and chatting informally.

I quickly went downstairs to nab a phone, with the only eyewitness account of Charlayne's first day of classes.

The integration had followed two hectic days in federal court in Atlanta, during which attorneys for Charlayne and Hamilton attacked the welter of excuses university officials had concocted to keep them out. Court rulings allowed the two to be the first to break Georgia's rigid barrier of absolute racial segregation from kindergarten to graduate school.

Charlayne was assigned to live in Center Myers Hall, the central dorm of three adjoining buildings, while Hamilton rented a room from a black family in Athens. A quiet young man with a warm smile, Hamilton planned to study medicine and had a four-year high school scholastic average of 3.88—equal to a 97 average on a 100 percentile scale.

He had told me that he felt he and Charlayne would encounter some trouble, but didn't anticipate too much from students, adding, "I think most of it will come from outside."

A large number of news people and students were waiting outside Charlayne's classroom building for her to walk out. Except for the crowd, it seemed just another day at the university.

Until that night.

Georgia had just lost a tight, emotion-packed basketball game 89-80 to archrival Georgia Tech in overtime, and a rowdy, jeering crowd began gathering.

The crowd, estimated at 1,000 to 2,000, began moving onto the campus near Charlayne's dorm to protest integration. I'd heard rumors that students would storm her dorm because they had heard there would be no police there and no risk of being expelled.

The crowd stopped in front of Charlayne's

ground-floor room, where faculty members, standing outside, requested that they leave. But the faculty group was shouted down by further jeering. Then the students began heaving bricks and Coke bottles toward Charlayne's window, breaking the glass. I was standing much farther back on the campus but could see huddled figures of girls looking out other windows.

The demonstrators, jeering and shouting, began yelling and chanting, "Nigger, go home," while two boys unfurled a bedsheet bearing the same words. Others threw rocks, empty bottles and hot coffee on news reporters and photographers and pitched firecrackers from the hillside.

Their chants were often vulgar and profane. One repeated shout was: "Two, four, six, eight... we don't want to integrate. Eight, six, four, two... we don't want no jiggerboo. Don't worry, nigger, the worst is yet to come. Don't worry, nigger."

I was standing next to a TV cameraman who was knocked down by a rock that struck him in the face. His camera was stolen while he was on the ground.

By then, police had arrived, and when the mob tried to rush the front doors of Charlayne's hall, they were held off by several dozen officers, along with hard-pressed university officials and teachers.

The action centered around William Tate, the university's dean of men, so I struggled to stay near him. Tate, burley and broad shouldered, was grabbing young guys by the shirt, demanding, "What's your name?" Then he confiscated their student ID cards.

Meanwhile, students threw matches into woods behind the dormitory, setting off brush fires that blazed away until firemen arrived and hosed down the dormitory and surrounding area.

At one point, firemen moved forward with fire hoses aimed at the rioters. Tate, a handful of teachers, a few other reporters and I followed them. The marauding students, seeing the large hose and expecting a powerful rush of water, fell back.

But when the hose was turned on, the water pressure was so weak that only a trickle flowed through. This brought on a roar from the rioters, who pushed forward again, while Tate and those of us behind him retreated rapidly.

News reporters, photographers and TV cameramen clumped in groups on the lawn, were caught between a cross fire of stones and fireworks. Several were in a nearby station wagon, and I joined them, all of us squeezed together, trying to dodge the mob.

One by one, we sneaked out of the car to get back to covering the riot. "Good luck," each whispered, crawling out.

Fights broke out when the police tried to arrest violent demonstrators, so they finally resorted to tear gas. But rioters grabbed the canisters and hurled them back.

White clouds of smoke rose in the night air, and the

crowd began to withdraw, people coughing and rubbing their eyes from the stinging gas. But rubbing your eyes only made them worse—as I soon found out.

A good-sized stone came flying through the air and struck me on the back of the head. At the same time, a tear gas canister grazed my face and dropped at my feet. The fumes quickly dried my throat, causing tears to stream down my face. I could hardly breathe or see.

Dizzy from the blow and gasping for breath, I rapped on the door of the dorm next to Charlayne's. A housemother opened it and asked, "Are you a student?"

"No," I stupidly replied, "a reporter."

At that, she said, "No reporters can come in," and slammed the door in my face.

Someone gathering up the injured hauled me off to a campus clinic. As soon as I was able to breathe better, I insisted on returning to the riot.

A doctor protested, but finally, with yellow salve smeared on my slightly burned face and throat, I signed myself out and caught a ride back to the action.

Frantically, I ran from house to house along the street, banging on doors and begging to use a phone. But with my hair flying about wildly, my face smeared with salve, and tear gas drifting in the air, few would open their doors. Those who did, once they saw me, slammed them shut. I remembered that a young Atlanta friend, Betty Routsos Kapetanakos, was attending the university with her husband and lived nearby.

I ran to her apartment. Betty let me in and, finally, I had a phone.

I quickly dialed AP in New York. The guys on the general desk, furious that they had not heard from their own reporters, had resorted to writing leads by watching TV.

When I finished dictating, I walked back to Charlayne's dorm. By then, the riot had fizzled. But the night air was still full of smoke and the acrid smell of tear gas. I suddenly realized I was alone on the lawn, overlooking the streets.

Spotting a station wagon jammed with TV men, I ran toward it as the car stopped and a back door was flung open while a man scrambled in. I yelled, "Hey, guys, it's me, Katy. Wait!" But they slammed the door and sped off.

I chased after them, but my TV friends, who'd been dodging stones and firecrackers and had their expensive cameras stolen and smashed, were too agitated to realize who I was. Undoubtedly, I was hardly recognizable.

Standing abandoned under a tree on the wide lawn, I wondered what I should do. Suddenly the branches of the tree shook. Out dropped AP photographer Horace Cort at my feet, camera in hand.

"Are you crazy?" Horace yelled. "What in hell are you doing out in the open? You're like a young second lieutenant who doesn't know crap! You could get killed! Don't you know how to take cover?" No, I didn't, but I was learning.

The hour was very late, but we decided to hang around just in case another demonstration sparked up.

Suddenly, a state patrol car pulled up, the front door of the dorm opened, and we spotted Charlayne being hurried out under escort.

We ran to the patrol car just as a tearful Charlayne got in. Horace was snapping away with his camera while I asked an officer what was going on.

He told us that Gov. Ernest Vandiver had suspended the two blacks "for their own protection and that of other students." Horace and I watched as the patrol whisked Charlayne off. Later, I learned that the troopers had also picked up Hamilton and driven both of them to their homes in Atlanta.

Horace drove back to our motel, and I phoned New York about the suspensions while he developed the photos. In those days on a major story, AP photographers often had to set up a darkroom in a bathroom of their motel to process film, since they needed water, electricity and darkness.

Suddenly, Horace, so excited he'd forgotten he was clad only in undershorts, ran down the hall and banged excitedly on my door. "Come quick, Katy," he said, "and see the picture I got!"

I was anxious to get some sleep but grabbed my robe and went to Horace's room. He ran into the bathroom, pushed aside the black plastic sheeting he'd used to keep the light out and triumphantly held up a dripping picture of Charlayne. It showed her crying and clutching a small Madonna as she climbed into the patrol car. In the dark outside, we had not seen that Charlayne, a Catholic, had been holding the religious statue under her coat.

That picture of a tearful Charlayne clutching a Madonna won front-page play the next morning in many newspapers, and I included that in my story on her suspension.

Later that day I had a telegram from our new Atlanta bureau chief, Bill Waugh, which read: "If I were there, I'd pin a dozen orchids on your shoulder. Congratulations on an excellent performance. Your copy has been as hot and timely as a tear gas bomb. Keep up the good work."

I hoped Horace had gotten praise, too. Almost singlehandedly, he had photographed numerous early civil rights clashes in the South and gotten exclusives for AP, just as he had on this one.

The next morning, reporters checked police records and found that eight of the 18 people arrested listed their ages as between 24 and 39—and admitted membership in the Klan. Later, the university announced that only 225 of its 7,400-member student body were involved in the rioting. Hundreds of others were spectators.

Charlayne and Hamilton's two lawyers—Constance Baker Motley and Donald Hollowell—appealed to Judge W. A. Bootle's U.S. District Court to reverse the suspensions and order them returned to their classes. More than half of the university's professors also insisted the two be allowed back in.

Five days later the federal court ordered Charlayne and Hamilton returned to the university, and students were given stern warnings against further lawless demonstrations. Their re-entry was peaceful, and after that night of violence, an academic air of tranquil adjustment to integration prevailed.

A few months later, the AP sent me back to the university to ask Charlayne and Hamilton how they were fitting in to campus life.

Driving past sorority homes, the towering Corinthian columns of antebellum days seemed solemn reminders of a way of life sharply broken by the two students who had endured racial hatred, violence and loneliness after they enrolled.

Both told me that their social lives were restricted and involved self-set curfews. "While we circulate freely around campus during the day, we rarely go out in the evening," Hamilton said.

Charlayne added, "Many students have gone out of their way to be cordial to us, but there is still considerable reserve from the majority." When they found the time, the two often drove the 70 miles to their Atlanta homes to spend weekends.

Two years later, both graduated, Charlayne with a degree in journalism. She was hired by The New York Times and later the New Yorker magazine. She subsequently went on to successful jobs at CNN and other television outlets.

Hamilton, elected to Phi Beta Kappa, graduated with academic distinction. The following fall he entered the Emory University School of Medicine in Atlanta, another first for his race. Asked how he felt about integration causes, he said, "When I came here, I was interested only in medicine. I'm still interested only in medicine. I won't become a crusader."

18

FACING OFF THE GUNS

THAT JUNE DAY IN 1963 when Gov. George Wallace made his defiant doorway stand at the University of Alabama was a sizzler—creeping miserably close to 100 degrees. And I, crouched on my knees under a table laden with microphones hiding from state troopers, felt even hotter.

I was only a few feet away from the entrance to the non-air-conditioned building—the only way I could cover the confrontation. There, the fiery segregationist governor stood blocking the attempt by U.S. Deputy Attorney General Nicholas Katzenbach to enroll two black students.

The University of Alabama was the nation's last university not yet racially integrated. That same year, marchers in Birmingham had been turned back with attack dogs and fire hoses as events swirled around Wallace.

Despite the scorching weather in Tuscaloosa, lawmen with rifles were stationed on top of the building where Wallace planned to make his defiant, stagecrafted doorway stand.

I'd flown to Tuscaloosa the day before and, as my taxi headed from the airport to a motel, the driver asked why I was going to the university. "I'm a reporter," I told him.

Then, he pulled a pistol and waving it toward me with his left hand on the wheel shouted, "If they start killing white people, I'll just start killing blacks." I did not answer, and he made no further comments but put his gun away.

As we neared the university, the campus was tightly sealed behind yellow wooden barricades, and blue-uniformed state troopers stopped the taxi to check my credentials. Troopers, keeping a sharp eye on any groups that might be forming, were patrolling in squad cars and thronging the entrance to the university.

The next day, as the climactic moment was approaching, the campus felt like an armed camp. The atmosphere, in spite of appeals from all sides for law and order, was electric with anxiety and excitement.

I joined dozens of reporters in the large auditorium in Foster Hall, a white-columned redbrick building where we'd been told there would be a "news" event.

Instead, state troopers suddenly pulled a fast one. To keep us from covering the dramatic confrontation between Wallace and Katzenbach, we were ignominiously locked inside the auditorium.

There was no news event. Alabama officials had simply used that as a ruse to get us into the room and keep us from getting out. I wasn't too worried, since I knew the AP had several reporters outside the building.

Inside, reporters were venting anger at the lockup. "What the hell?" I heard over and over. I was listening to several guys who were planning how to break out when I heard my name paged on the loudspeaker.

I went to the door, where an Alabama state trooper handed me a note scribbled by AP's Montgomery correspondent, Rex Thomas, whose son happened to be an Alabama trooper. The note read: "They won't let us within 300 feet of the doorway. You'll have to cover for us."

I assumed that Rex did not know our frantic situation. How to get out when the entrances were guarded? I walked up to the trooper at one doorway and told him I had to go to the bathroom.

The young blond officer, his face blushing, stammered that he had orders not to let anyone out. I kept pleading, and he finally gave in. "OK," he told me. "But only if you give your word that you'll return."

Crossing my fingers behind my back, I promised. Then, fearful that I might run into other troopers, I scampered down the empty hall to the front steps of Foster Hall, where Katzenbach and two U.S. marshals had escorted the black students for their court-ordered registration.

There stood a grim-faced Wallace, flanked by

helmeted state troopers, adamantly refusing to admit the two 20-year-olds, Vivian Malone and James Hood.

At that time, I did not know that the violence was somewhat staged, or that a few newsmen outside had apparently convinced the governor to allow them close enough to hear. I still thought I was the only reporter trying to cover the words spoken during an historic confrontation.

I'd spotted a table next to the door, obviously placed there earlier for broadcast and news reporters, who had loaded it with microphones and other equipment. Now, though, they were locked in the auditorium.

Troopers were hovering around Wallace, and I was concerned they might spot me. But they were staring intently at the governor and Katzenbach. That gave me a chance to sneak under the heavily laden table without being noticed.

In the South, in a profession predominantly male at the time, being a woman, and small, helped make me practically invisible to authority figures.

Crouched under the table, I could see the trouser legs of Wallace and Katzenbach only a few feet away. Pulling out my notebook and pen, I began scribbling down their conversation. Although staring at their shoes, I could easily tell who was saying what by their voices.

Wallace, in a symbolic attempt to block the two black students, cited the constitutional right of states to operate public schools, colleges and universities. He then refused the enrollment of the two students.

Katzenbach, whose legs were shaking, asked Wallace to reconsider, saying he was violating a federal court order. He also told the governor that he carried a proclamation from President Kennedy, calling for obedience to the order.

Three times the defiant Alabama governor refused to budge, saying he was on hand as he had vowed for weeks that he would be, "to prevent the entrance because it is illegal and unwarranted."

The federal officials then left the doorway and drove the two students to their assigned dormitories to wait for Kennedy's solution to the crisis. I crept out from under the table and slipped down the long hallway, where I spotted a lone telephone booth and ducked in to phone the AP.

At that time, if you could not give the operator the number you were calling from, you could not place a long-distance call. A phone was our only resource for filing a story, and a wire service reporter, in particular, needed to be able to get breaking news out as swiftly as possible. I memorized the number, then scratched it out, a dirty trick but the only way I could prevent other reporters from grabbing it.

I kept the phone open long-distance to my office. Meanwhile, a state trooper striding down the long hall saw me in the booth and stopped. "Out," he ordered. "Out of the building!"

I refused and he pulled his pistol, pointing it at me. I wasn't afraid. I knew he wouldn't shoot, but I said, "OK, I'll leave," and began slowly gathering my notes together from the floor and shelf of the booth. When the trooper began walking away, I resumed dictating.

President Kennedy then federalized the Alabama National Guard, taking it out of Wallace's control. He authorized the Defense Department to use whatever troops might be necessary to allow the two blacks to be enrolled.

For the rest of the blistering summer afternoon, I was dashing up and down four short flights of stairs, watching Alabama troops march on campus, then running back to the phone to dictate on my open line. At the end of the day, I'd lost four pounds from running on stairs in the sultry heat.

The "segregation forever" barrier raised by Wallace fell without a shot fired. The governor had put on his promised "standing in the schoolhouse door" act by barring the students that morning, but he made no effort to resist the might of the federal government.

Brig. Gen. Henry Graham informed Wallace it was his "sad duty" to report that the Alabama National Guard was now under federal control. Wallace commented it was a "bitter pill" for the state's guardsmen to have to enforce desegregation, then climbed into a car and rode away.

With green-clad National Guardsmen on the alert, the registration of the blacks came almost as an anti-climax. Malone, clad in a pink summer frock, and Hood, in a dark gray suit, quietly walked into the building, escorted by federal officials, paid their fees and registered.

Thus a last citadel of all-out segregation in the United States fell. Alabama had been the only state in the union without at least token integration of some public educational facilities.

Malone, who planned to study business administration, and Hood, a psychology student, told reporters they hoped to get down to their purpose: study.

That night, I was in a Tuscaloosa drugstore to buy bandages for the blisters I'd gotten running up and down the stairs and saw Katzenbach there for the same reason, buying balm for his aching feet. We exchanged greetings and laughed about our mutual drugstore mission.

Later, I was to learn that Wallace's obstructive stand was mostly symbolic, a Southern politician promising something he knew he could not deliver. Wallace had been vanquished by a prearranged show of force. The news media learned that the governor's aides had privately informed Kennedy that Wallace wanted a show of barring the students, but not a showdown.

That, apparently, was why Kennedy had nationalized the Alabama National Guard and sent them to "force" Wallace to admit the students. The governor's doorway stand was memorable, but futile.

Only eight days later, with Alabama's integration fresh before the eyes of the nation, Kennedy introduced the new civil rights bill, the most sweeping such legislation in America's history.

Though President Kennedy was assassinated in November 1963, the bill survived an 83-day filibuster and was pushed through the Congress in 1964 by President Lyndon Johnson to become the law of the land.

The university crisis catapulted Wallace into the national spotlight, and he would begin his first presidential campaign in 1964, in Wisconsin.

19

MOONING THE MEDIA

One steamy summer day in the mid-'60s, I was among those sent to cover a SNCC demonstration in Atlanta, only to find ourselves suddenly locked into an empty warehouse over old railroad tracks, in an area of downtown known as "the Gulch."

SNCC leaders herded reporters and photographers into a stuffy, airless room on the upper level of the warehouse, allegedly for the news conference. Then we heard a click at the door. We were locked inside.

We were hot, sweating and grumbling about our plight. One reporter, irate that we were being held against our will, got the idea of having the guys take off their shirts, tying them into a rope and then lowering me—the only female in the room and weighing about 100 pounds—out a window to the ground to go for help.

That idea got as far as a few of the men tying their shirts together when members of SNCC, apparently observing us through the keyhole, unlocked the door.

At another SNCC demonstration downtown, I was

with reporters gathered on the sidewalk, throwing fast questions at Stokely Carmichael, a flamboyant civil rights activist. A native of Trinidad, Carmichael in 1966 had seized the SNCC leadership from John Lewis, one of its founders and a believer in nonviolence.

Carmichael, early on a young idealist, now was voicing dissatisfaction with King's peaceful achievements. As we questioned Carmichael on the sidewalk, he suddenly displayed an overt show of contempt for the media by dropping his trousers to his ankles.

I was the only female in the group, and Carmichael, clad in his undershorts, glanced over at me and said courteously, "Excuse me, ma'am." Knowing Carmichael's sharp tongue and hostility to whites, I was surprised by his unexpected politeness.

Another time during those demanding, unforgettable years, I was plodding along a county road in Georgia with a silent, dispirited group of marchers under a broiling summer sun. Heat and fatigue were getting to everyone.

I was trying to organize a story in my head so I could file—that is, if I could dash to a nearby home and ask to use their phone, if they had one. Most of the homes we passed were unpainted shacks and shanties just off the highway. I needed to unload my story then run to catch up with the marchers.

Suddenly, a 6-foot-tall woman who towered over the others began singing in a powerful voice the defiant spiritual "Ain't Gonna Let Nobody Turn Me Round, Turn Me Round."

Other marchers, swaying arm in arm, joined in, and when that ended, another voice would sing out the start of another spiritual. By the time they got to "We Shall Overcome," the march, guided by the woman's overpowering voice and vibrant spirit, had regained its vitality.

That march was one of many, gradually melding the Movement into a cause, a social revolution unlike anything America had experienced since the Civil War.

20

STUCK IN THE BALCONY

On a sultry summer day in August 1964, as the South was seething with violence, a chilling murder case was about to be tried in the northeast Georgia town of Danielsville.

The victim, Lt. Col. Lemuel Penn, a U.S. Army Reserve officer, was black. The jury was all white and all male, the courtroom racially segregated, and the two men on trial members of the Ku Klux Klan.

The previous year, the infamous Klan slayings of three young civil rights workers, two white men and one black, occurred in Neshoba County, Mississippi. After months of searching, their bodies were found buried in an earthen dam. Medgar Evers, Mississippi field secretary for the NAACP, was shot to death by a sniper, and four young black girls, preparing for a Youth Rally service, died when a bomb blasted the 16th Street Baptist Church in Birmingham.

The Penn killing on July 11 came just nine days after the signing of the Civil Rights Act of 1964—during a period in America's history when blacks were being brutally beaten and lynched. Klan activity had surged in the Deep South after the civil rights bill was passed, in a bloody battle to maintain a segregated society.

A cruel double standard existed for blacks, long grossly mistreated by the criminal justice system. That was particularly true in murder cases.

Penn, a 49-year-old decorated veteran of World War II and assistant superintendent of schools in Washington, D.C., had been heading home with two other black officers. They had just completed an annual tour of duty at Fort Benning and, aware of racial tension in the area and that it would be time-consuming to search for an all-black hotel or boarding house, they planned to drive all night on back roads.

After stopping in Athens, Georgia, to change drivers, Penn was driving along a lonely, mist-shrouded road on the Madison County line. A car suddenly pulled next to his and slowed. Shots were fired. Half of Penn's face was blown off.

Fifty-one days later, three Klansmen were charged in the wanton killing. President Johnson, notified of Penn's murder, had ordered the FBI onto the case. The head of the FBI in Athens, aware of the activities of troublemakers and their threats against blacks, suggested that the investigation focus on men identified as Klansmen: Joseph Howard Sims, Robert Myers, James Lackey and Herbert Guest.

A grand jury was convened and murder indictments returned against Sims, Myers and Lackey. Guest was charged as an accessory after the fact, but not indicted. Their arrests came on evidence an FBI agent said he obtained by attending a Klan meeting undercover.

On the day the trial began at the Madison County Courthouse, the lawn was festive looking. A large colorful umbrella blossomed on top of refreshment stand, set up by the Ladies Auxiliary of the Veterans of Foreign Wars.

Dozens of reporters had descended on the small town, and a sensational court trial was great theater. The auxiliary women were hawking sandwiches and cold lemonade. I mingled with the media guys, sipping a Coke while waiting impatiently for the courtroom doors to open.

When they opened, I showed officials my press card and was directed outside and upstairs to the balcony. I had to duck to avoid the low ceiling before stepping in. I was so absorbed, so focused on the important trial that it did not immediately strike me that I was sent upstairs because I was female.

I sat down and, looking around the darkened balcony traditionally reserved for blacks, I noticed I was the sole white person. Seated nearby were some 20 black men, clad in overalls. I thought then about the movie "To Kill a Mockingbird," a film released a few years earlier that captured the awful brutality against blacks.

I realized that blacks were not alone in being

discriminated against: so were women. My instinct was to protest, and I started back downstairs, ready to complain. Then it struck me that any arguing on my part would only give officials an excuse to bounce me from the courthouse. And I was the only AP reporter covering the trial.

After all, that was the way journalists in general were treated by many Southern officials at that time. My fear of being banned from the trial overcame my justifiable anger, and I turned around and climbed back upstairs.

Discrimination, as I was discovering, was aimed at female reporters, who, according to some rural officials, had no business covering court trials anyway. When the official at the door was checking my press pass, he frowned and muttered, "Little lady, you oughta be home, looking after family!"

For three weeks, I had to cover the trial by peering over the railing of the tiny, stifling-hot balcony in the old, non-air-conditioned courthouse.

When the judge walked to the bench and gaveled for order, courtroom chatter ceased. You could sense the silent tension of the more than 200 spectators packing the courtroom.

For the first time in Madison County, two blacks were among the 96 males called for a jury pool. But their names were quickly struck by the defense, along with any man who subscribed to The Atlanta Journal,

The Atlanta Constitution or the Columbia (S.C.) Record.

Finally, a panel of 12 white male jurors, mostly middle-aged farmers, merchants and laborers, all wearing white shirts, no jackets, was seated.

Rough-cut colorful language spilled out in Solicitor General Clete Johnson's opening statement. "These night riders struck at this unsuspecting victim and then sped away just like a snake slithering in the grass." Calling the killing a "horrible thing," Johnson demanded the death penalty. He warned that if the jurors condoned the killing of Penn, human life had "less value than a 10-cent box of snuff."

One of the first witnesses was Maj. Charles Brown, who was in the car with Penn that night. He testified that he and the two other officers were returning from duty at Fort Benning. Brown was asleep in the right front seat when two shots were fired. At first, he thought they had blown two tires.

"Then, I saw Colonel Penn's head slumped on his chest," Brown said. "His hands were not on the steering wheel. I felt something hot on my left arm. It turned out to be blood."

Brown then told how he and Lt. Col. John Howard moved Penn's body from beneath the steering wheel and managed to turn the car around on the Broad River Bridge and head back toward Athens. But their car then spun off the road and ran into a ditch.

Scrambling out, the two climbed the grassy bank and Brown tried to flag down a passing motorist. "Help us if you can. Someone has been killed!" he yelled to the driver. The car slowed, turned around and went back in the direction of Athens. It returned later accompanied by another car with a law enforcement officer.

Asked why they had turned the car around, Brown said, "If you had been hit by weapons and were not armed with anything to defend yourself, I don't think you'd continue in the same direction as those lights we saw in the fog."

Howard testified that he was in the backseat when he saw a cream-colored car swerve around just after the gunfire. Later, Dr. Larry Howard of the Georgia State Crime Laboratory testified that Penn was killed by a shotgun, the shots fired from another car.

A state witness, 18-year-old Thomas "Hossfly" Folendore, testified that he saw Sims, a heavyset 41-year-old man, and Myers, a tall, thin, dark-haired 25-year-old, carrying sawed-off shotguns into Herbert Guest's garage in Athens soon after the time of the slaying. The defense countered with two alibi defendants who placed Sims and Myers at an all-night Athens café during the time of the murder.

Over heated objections from the defense, the FBI read a signed statement from Lackey, who was driving the car. It said Sims had spotted the District of

Columbia tag on Penn's car and said, "That must be some of President Johnson's boys. I'm gonna kill me a nigger."

The men tailed the car carrying the Army men out of Athens. Then, Lackey's statement said, "both Sims and Myers told me when to pass the car. When I was alongside, both Sims and Myers fired shotguns into the Negroes' car." Lackey insisted he did not know they really meant to shoot and, when he learned of Penn's death, his statement read, "I said to myself, those sonsabitches killed that man."

Jim Hudson, the young defense attorney, countered that Lackey had since repudiated the confession and quoted the service station attendant as saying he repudiated it because of "my mental condition at the time [of the murder]."

Hudson called on an Atlanta psychiatrist, who testified that Lackey had a borderline low IQ of 90 and described Lackey as a "paranoid personality type."

Prosecution attorneys then threw a second incriminating statement at Myers and Sims. In a signed statement taken by FBI agents, Guest had quoted both men as telling him two days after Penn's death that "they were the ones that shot at the car."

The statement said the two had intended "to scare away any out-of-town Negroes" who might stir up trouble because "we had heard that Martin Luther

King might make Georgia a testing ground for the civil rights bill." Guest's statement corroborated much of what Lackey had told the FBI.

A heavyset, curly-haired man with several bottom front teeth missing, Guest was called as a state witness and swore that he did not know what he had told the FBI: "I blacked out and I don't remember anything."

After days of incriminating testimony and rebuttals, the attorneys rested their case. Judge Carey Skelton recessed the proceedings at the request of a defense attorney due to the late hour. The judge, obviously weary, told the court, "I'm going home tonight and go possum hunting."

Every day, for three weeks, I had leaned over the stifling-hot balcony with several dozen blacks, all of us intent on hearing the procedures. We were often wiping sweat from our faces. Down below, I could see Sims' wife with their eight children and Myers' pregnant wife with their three young sons.

Since so many reporters were in Danielsville, Judge Skelton, a stocky, gray-haired man, suddenly found himself in the spotlight and was not happy. He had banned cameras and recording equipment from the courtroom and even prohibited news pictures from being shot on the courthouse lawn.

During a lunch break, AP photographer Horace Cort, trying to shoot a picture from the street, made the mistake of placing his foot on the concrete curb around the courthouse lawn. A policeman spotted him.

Horace explained that he'd barely put his foot on the curb and was only trying to get a better camera shot. Standing nearby, I could tell that Horace's efforts were doomed, and the officer arrested him for contempt.

I went immediately to the judge's office to protest. The judge was not in, and I asked a clerk where Horace was being held. "In a jail close by," he told me.

I started a quick run across the courthouse lawn, looking for the jail and calling loudly, "Horace! Horace, where are you?"

In the tiny nearby jail cell, Horace yelled, "Katy! I'm here! In jail! Get me out!"

I hurried back to the courthouse to track down Judge Skelton. This time he was in his office, and I told him I was present when Horace was arrested, that he had only put his foot on the curb to better position his camera.

The judge had Horace brought before him and Horace apologized for his misstep. The judge, no doubt concerned about heavy national press coverage, dismissed the charge.

I had my problems, too, from sitting in the balcony. I had to dash down two short flights of stairs several times each day, dodging traffic while running across the street—the old courthouse was in the middle of the town square—then track down and nab the nearest of the few phones in town.

21

RAFTER-RINGING PLEAS

On the last day of the trial, after the state had built a huge mass of evidence to prove that Sims and Myers had killed Penn, the defense had only taken several hours to present its case. Myers and Sims each took the stand under an old Georgia law—since declared unconstitutional—that allowed them to make unsworn statements without cross-examination.

Myers, a textile worker, stood up and told the jury, "I'm the father of three children, and I'm expecting another one soon. I can assure you I had nothing to do with the killing of Lemuel Penn." Sims also declared he had nothing to do with Penn's death.

In closing statements, prosecutors and defense lawyers alike made impassioned pleas. Defense attorney Jim Hudson said in a loud voice, "This ain't no car-theft case, and this ain't no guitar-picking-on-Sunday case. This is a murder case."

Then, in a Southern country lawyer's appeal to

human instincts, he called for "pity" toward the two Klansmen. "Don't send them to the electric chair in Reidsville, into those cold gray walls—and the lights get dim—don't do it on such evidence as this," Hudson pleaded, pounding the railing of the jury box. A lock of dark blond hair fell across his forehead as he shouted, "You can't, after you electrocute them—and their children ain't got no daddy—come back and say you wonder if they did it!"

Another court-appointed defense lawyer, John Darsey, made a fiery plea for acquittal, hammering at the racial issue and the federal government. The 60-year-old Darsey never mentioned the evidence in the case, but in an hourlong racist argument, shouted, while slapping the railing of the jury box, that the administration had loosed "a horde of federal agents in our midst."

Lowering his voice, he added: "President Johnson sent them swarming into Madison County." Then, in a rafter-ringing, arm-waving argument that left him soaking with perspiration, Darsey said that FBI agents had been instructed to "go to Madison County and don't come back until you bring us white meat!"

The "social revolution," Darsey added, had plagued the nation with "sit-ins, sit-downs, walk-ins, walk-outs, insurrections, riots, police dogs, fire hoses, U.S. marshals and federal troops.

"They may succeed in passing forced laws," he

shouted in a rising voice. "They may get them upheld and ruled constitutional by the U.S. Supreme Court. They may break down the distinction between federal jurisdiction and states' rights. But in the name of all that's holy," he yelled, "they shall never destroy the jury system, which is the heart and soul of Anglo-Saxon jurisprudence!"

Pacing back and forth in front of the jury, Darsey continued, his voice reverberating through the courtroom. "Never let it be said that a Madison County jury converted an electric chair into a sacrificial altar on which the pure flesh of a member of the human race was sacrificed—to the savage revengeful appetite of a raging mob!"

Wringing his hands and mopping his brow, Darsey reminded the jury they were Anglo-Saxon and, while charging that the federal government had set out specifically to get Sims and Myers, his voice pitching to a scream, shouted, "Fe fi fo fum! I smell the blood of an Englishman! Send 'em on, Mister President, send 'em on!"

Scribbling those final fiery arguments as fast as I could into my reporter's notebook, I realized they were bound to make dramatic national copy.

Even the old courtroom, with its age lines, drab cracks in the wall and time-worn benches, offered a classic setting for drama. On the floor in front of the jurors were old, dented brass spittoons, polished to a shine. Occasionally, a juror missed aim as he spat chewing tobacco but when he scored a hit, even those of us in the balcony could hear a soft distinct "plink."

Solicitor General Johnson quietly and calmly told the jurors that the state had proved beyond any reasonable doubt that the defendants murdered Penn. He asked for the death penalty, saying Penn was slain "with a motive of hate and violence."

"Lemuel Penn was born a Negro," Johnson said. "He came into this world with a black skin. Is that a crime? Would that justify taking a shotgun and blowing his head off because he is black?"

Jeff Wayne, the special prosecutor, then took the floor, saying, "Our laws are not made for the protection of one color or one race. Except for the grace of God, you could have been born of the colored race."

The jury, which had been sitting impassively during the trial, retired at 4:40 p.m. on Friday, Sept. 4, and began deliberating.

After two hours, the jurors piled into Georgia State Patrol cars to dine at a truck stop several miles out of town. Fearful of losing sight of the jurors, I drove along with another reporter to the same truck stop to eat.

Strangely enough, all of us, newsmen, jurors, lawyers and judge, were seated at the same long table for dinner, which was the only large table in the diner.

Together—with a jury under deliberations—we

ate a Southern country meal of fried chicken, french fries, mashed potatoes, coleslaw and sweetened iced tea. We talked about the scorching weather and other topics—anything but the trial. At the head of our table sat the gray-haired judge, who looked troubled and rarely spoke a word.

After dinner, we all drove back to the courthouse, the jurors resumed deliberating and I took my lone seat in the balcony. I did not wonder why any of the blacks who had been sitting with me hadn't returned. Systematically oppressed for so long, they did not expect justice. And they knew better than to stay for the verdict.

I arranged with an elderly couple who lived across from the courthouse to have a phone handy for the verdict. I'd noticed the couple sitting each evening in rocking chairs on their front porch, watching the crowds. I gave them a $20 bill and a large box of chocolates to let me open their lone phone line to my Atlanta office. I also gave them my business card and asked that they let me know my long-distance charges after their bill came. I'd called my office when it seemed we'd have a verdict shortly and told the staffer to keep my phone line open. Then I placed the phone down sideways on a small table.

Soon after 10 o'clock, the judge sent word that a verdict had been reached. The hot, crowded, jabbering courtroom audience turned suddenly silent. The clerk read the verdict handed him by the jury foreman:

"We, the jury, find the defendants, Joseph Howard Sims and Cecil Myers, not guilty."

A gasp and loud murmur rose from the courtroom along with shouts and clapping, and the judge rapped for order. I leaped down the balcony steps three at a time, dashed across the street just as a huge truck was rounding the street circling the courthouse. I could hear screeching as the driver hit his brakes and did his best to miss me. Later, I discovered the truck had slightly touched my skirt—it was smeared with grease.

I ran to the house where I'd left the open phone, dashed down the long hall and phoned in the verdict. The AP had a substantial beat!

Only then did I have time to think about the verdict—which was an outrageous travesty of justice. Despite overwhelming evidence of guilt during the five-day trial, the two defendants were found not guilty.

Sims and Myers both still faced federal civil rights charges of conspiring to threaten, injure, oppress, intimidate or kill Negroes in order to keep them from exercising their civil rights. Four days after their acquittal, they were released on $25,000 bail each.

Guest, who had been freed earlier of murder charges,

was arrested with the other men for conspiring to violate Penn's civil rights.

Lackey, still facing murder and civil rights conspiracy charges, was unable to make bail and remained in jail until Jan. 7, 1965. He was finally released on $10,000 bail and was never tried on the murder count.

On June 28, 1968, Sims and Myers were brought into the federal courtroom in Athens. They were to stand trial again on conspiracy charges of trying to keep out-of-state blacks from coming into the Athens area or trying to run them out by intimidation. Both were found guilty and sentenced to 10 years each in the federal penitentiary.

After serving his time, Sims was again in court, pleading guilty to assault with intent to kill his estranged wife, and was given another 10-year sentence. While in prison, both men were divorced by their wives. Fifteen years after Penn's murder, Myers and Sims were free, but in June of 1981, Sims was shot to death by a friend who blasted him with a shotgun at a flea market near Athens.

Penn, the father of two children, had never been involved in civil rights. He was murdered because his car had a Washington, D.C., license plate and his skin was black.

Years later, I was taking part in a seminar at one of Atlanta's black colleges when a reporter from

Newsweek mentioned that during the Penn trial reporters had been assigned to a reserved downstairs section on the right side of the courtroom.

"Reserved! Downstairs! They sent me upstairs!" I exclaimed from the podium. I knew other reporters were downstairs but not that they were in a reserved section. I told the audience how I'd been officially directed to the gallery, presumably because I was female. Young blacks in the audience, understanding discrimination well, roared with laughter.

The killers of Lemuel Penn were quickly nabbed and charged, but many murders during civil rights years remain unsolved cold cases. Reporters now are reopening old cases from that era when blacks "rightfully feared the KKK and the fire bombings, abductions, castrations, rapes and murders," says Hank Klibanoff, co-author with Gene Roberts of "The Race Beat: The Press, the Civil Rights Struggle, and the Awakening of a Nation," and managing editor of the Civil Rights Cold Case Project. "The cold cases we're pursuing belong to a genre of criminality that went beyond a few disconnected acts of violence."

In Nieman Reports (Fall 2011), Klibanoff says that they "identify violent Klansmen who operated with the knowledge of law enforcement, legislators, mayors and governors, often with their participation and protection.

"The Klan—and its virulent spinoffs—was organized homegrown terrorism, more pervasive, damaging and deadly than anything this nation has known."

Klibanoff says that "black families who lived in the South at that time still do not know who killed their father, mother, grandfather, niece, brother or sister. The families are not seeking revenge, they just want to know."

This aerial view shows crowds at the Lincoln Memorial in Washington, during Martin Luther King Jr.'s "I Have a Dream" speech on Aug. 28, 1963. (AP Photo)

U.S. President Lyndon B. Johnson, right, talks with civil rights leaders in his White House office in Washington, D.C., Jan. 18, 1964. The black leaders, from left, are Roy Wilkins, James Farmer, Dr. Martin Luther King Jr., and Whitney Young. (AP Photo)

King talks to a reporter as he joins the picket line at the Scripto plant in Atlanta, Ga., in support of striking employees, Dec. 19, 1964. (AP Photo)

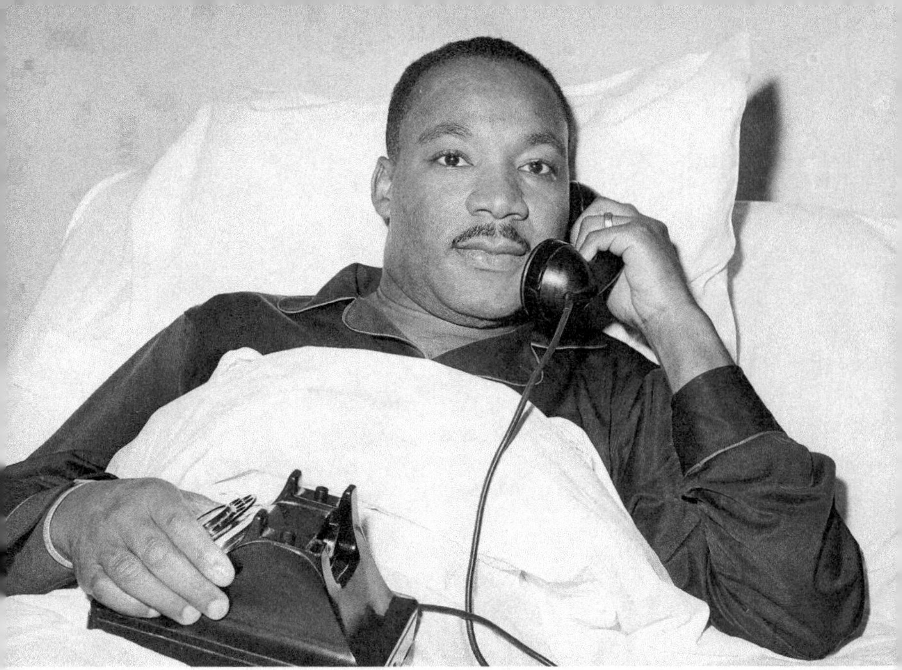

Integration leader Dr. Martin Luther King Jr. receives word by phone that he has been awarded the Nobel Peace Prize as he lies in a hospital bed in Atlanta, Ga., Oct. 14, 1964, where he went for a checkup. (AP Photo)

Rev. Martin Luther King with his wife, Coretta, participate in march from Montgomery, Ga., to the state capitol on March 19, 1965. (AP Photo)

Kathryn interviewing Coretta Scott King in her office in Atlanta, Ga., 1968. (Kathryn Johnson Collection)

Coretta Scott King and her son, Martin Luther King III, "Marty," sometime in the early 1970s. (Kathryn Johnson Collection)

Kathryn dictating a story from Sen. Richard Russell's funeral, Atlanta, Ga., Jan. 1971. (Kathryn Johnson Collection)

Georgia Democratic fifth district congressional candidate Andrew Young thanks campaign workers at Atlanta headquarters, Wednesday, Sept. 10, 1970 and draws a laugh from Coretta Scott King. (AP Photo)

Kathryn with Andrew Young shortly after she was appointed as a Nieman Fellow at Harvard, 1976. (Kathryn Johnson Collection)

Kathryn in the AP bureau office in Atlanta, Ga., 1978.
(Kathryn Johnson Collection)

Kathryn at her typewriter in the AP bureau office in Atlanta, Ga., sometime in the late 1970s. (Kathryn Johnson Collection)

Kathryn, now retired, shown at her home in the Virginia Highlands section of Atlanta, Ga., on July 16, 2015. (AP Photo/Valerie Komor)

22

BLOODY SUNDAY IN SELMA

THE STUDENT NONVIOLENT COORDINATING Committee had been working for two years to register blacks in Selma, Alabama, which had a history of entrenched white supremacy. Almost as many blacks as whites lived in the small town of 30,000, yet only 2 percent were registered voters.

Young blacks, ready to march for voting rights in the spring of 1965, planned to walk the 54 miles from Selma to Montgomery, to take their case before Gov. George Wallace.

The governor issued an order prohibiting the march but marchers gathered at Brown's Chapel—headquarters for the Movement—then began walking.

Nearby was a posse led by Jim Clark, the tough-talking racist sheriff of Dallas County. On his lapel, he wore a pin with the word "never," his response to the black effort for voting rights.

As the marchers crossed the steel-arched Edmund Pettus Bridge spanning the muddy Alabama River, state troopers stood just short of the bridge. Ordered to disperse, the marchers stood still—it took raw courage to face what was coming.

Suddenly, lawmen on horseback, led by Sheriff Clark, joined state troopers, wearing gas masks and carrying billy clubs. Together, they swept in a wave over the unarmed marchers.

Screaming and gasping, their eyes streaming, the marchers broke across an open field, chased by officers on horseback swinging clubs and striking the marchers, some of whom had knelt in prayer. That beating cracked the skull of John Lewis, a young activist who then headed SNCC and later became a U.S. congressman—and a civil rights icon.

The police clubbing, caught by TV on a Sunday night and dubbed "Bloody Sunday," shocked viewers across America. People were horrified at what they were seeing.

At home, watching on TV, I felt a sense of pathos that something so brutal could be taking place in our country.

That order by Wallace to stop the march, along with photo, TV and news coverage, became the catalyst that brought on the historic Selma March.

King had already planned such a march but had pushed back the date and left for Atlanta to preach that Sunday. However, King knew well when to take advantage of public opinion, and announced that a second Selma march would take place on March 21.

Drawn by the dramatic events at the bridge, outsiders, college students, priests, nuns, ministers and others began flocking into Alabama.

National opinion also had begun veering on the side of civil rights after the Freedom Rides and the Klan bombing of a church in Birmingham, which took the lives of four young black girls.

King put out a call to clergy and rabbis over the nation to join. Among those arriving were the Rev. James Reeb, a Unitarian minister from Boston, and two other white ministers. The three had had dinner at a black café and were walking out when they were brutally beaten by white men. Reeb died a few days later without regaining consciousness.

That event, too, horrified most Americans and soon, gaining voting rights became the focus of the marches. The Civil Rights Act of 1964, with all its significance, had not ensured blacks the right to register to vote.

Two weeks after Bloody Sunday, the Selma March—that most incredible of all racial demonstrations in the South—began.

President Johnson ordered the Alabama National Guard on active duty and sent regular Army riot forces, members of the FBI and federal marshals to protect the marchers.

Writers from the AP in New York flew to Selma, while Atlanta sent staffers, including me, back and forth to Selma as needed.

While driving to Selma on the first day of the march, I passed huge segregationist billboards and arrived just as a straggly little group was beginning. A few barefoot white girls ran alongside the marchers, shouting encouragement while a lone helicopter hovered overhead.

As the days wore on, blacks, barefoot and in tattered clothes, came in from shacks and cotton fields to be part of the march. Celebrities, students, priests, nuns, rabbis and ministers of all faiths flew into Alabama to join. A woman was there in a wheelchair. A few white hecklers stood alongside the highway, their favorite target a one-legged white man. As the man moved slowly on crutches, hecklers shouted, "left, left, left," for cadence.

I spoke briefly with a few whites in the march and could tell by their accents they were Southerners. Few people nationwide seemed to realize that millions of Southerners deplored violence. Perhaps that was due to the complexity of the civil rights movement.

During the next five days, hundreds tramped past rolling farms and pasturelands, through swamps and creeks in sweltering weather. Evenings, they sang freedom songs and ate their dinner off paper plates while sitting on the ground. Nights, they slept in big tents thrown up at designated points along the roadside.

As the march neared an end, rain was pouring so frequently that they camped in a rain-soaked pasture, flinging themselves down, exhausted, under the tents.

On the eve of the entry into Montgomery, marchers enjoyed a huge "entertainment extravaganza" night, featuring top stage and screen celebrities. Black entertainer Sammy Davis Jr. canceled the evening performance of "Golden Boy" on Broadway to take part.

King had left the march briefly but joined again later. On the last day, eight abreast, thousands pressed forward in a stream of humanity for nearly 2 miles. Reaching Montgomery, they marched around the Capitol to the beat of "The Battle Hymn of the Republic"—the marching song of Union forces in the Civil War.

The old capital of the Confederacy, as Montgomery was known, looked like an occupied military zone as hundreds of battle-ready National Guardsmen and Army regulars patrolled Dexter Avenue, the broad main street leading up to the Capitol.

The crowds had mushroomed to an estimated 25,000 when King spoke from the marble steps of the Capitol. From those same steps, Jefferson Davis had stood during the Civil War to accept the oath of office as president of the Confederate States of America. And from there, Wallace had shouted on his inauguration as governor two years earlier, "Segregation now! Segregation tomorrow! Segregation forever!"

King told the jubilant marchers, "I know some of you are asking today, 'How long will it take?' It will not be long. Because truth pressed to earth will rise again.

How long? Not long, because no lie can live forever..." Then, "Glory hallelujah! Glory hallelujah!"

Driving back to Atlanta, I was so exhausted I tried to stay awake by rolling the car window down to let air blow on my face. I'd not had a decent night's sleep or a hot meal for days. Driving back with me was an exhausted AP reporter who had fallen asleep on the backseat. After an hour, I pulled over to the side of the highway and reached back to shake him so he could take over the wheel, but I couldn't wake him.

I kept on driving—and much too fast, since I, too, was very sleepy. Ordinarily, I'd have worried about speeding, but I knew that most Alabama state troopers were in Montgomery.

Finally, we were in Atlanta, and after dropping off my colleague, I drove home and took the phone off the hook. "I don't care if Alabama is blown off the map," I told Mother. "Don't wake me."

The next morning, however, Mother replaced the phone, and it soon rang. I was ordered back to work: 39-year-old Viola Liuzzo, a housewife and mother of five, had been shot and killed.

Mrs. Liuzzo, a white volunteer for the civil rights cause, had made a "conscience" trip to Alabama from her home in Detroit, to help drive marchers back to Montgomery. She was driving a young black boy back to Montgomery after the march ended and paid for that with a bullet in the head.

Mrs. Liuzzo's murder was a shocking end to the historic march, which had also ended without a voting rights petition being presented to Wallace, who had declared repeatedly that he would not receive any delegation of "outside agitators."

Still, the march was highly successful. Only four and a half months later, President Johnson signed into law the Voting Rights Act of 1965, a sweeping piece of legislation guaranteeing the right to vote and transforming the lives of blacks.

23

BLACK POWER

Young black activist Willie Ricks, standing on the back of a flatbed truck in Greenwood, Mississippi, in 1966, spoke of white blood flowing then began shouting, "Black power!"

Almost immediately, those words were seized upon and given potency by Stokely Carmichael, only one month in office as head of SNCC.

The militant use of the slogan "Black Power" frightened many whites, who were just beginning to acknowledge civil rights.

SNCC had begun as a mixed black and white student organization, but Carmichael, disenchanted and impatient with the way things were going, made it known that whites were no longer wanted in SNCC. He had become increasingly bitter after the bodies of three of his voting rights activist friends—James Earl Chaney from Meridian, Mississippi, and Andrew Goodman and Michael Schwerner, both of New York City—had been found buried in an earthen dam in Mississippi, victims of the Klan.

Standing on a platform at a rally in Mississippi,

Carmichael, now a firebrand, told the crowd he'd been arrested "27 times, and I ain't going to jail no more.

"The only way," Carmichael said, "of stopping white men from whupping us is to take over. We been saying 'freedom' for six years, and we ain't got nothing. What we gonna start saying now is 'black power.'"

The crowd picked up the slogan and began chanting it.

Heard countless times across America, the slogan was praised for bringing new vigor to the Movement but blamed for "white backlash" as well as splitting the civil rights movement.

At first, King told the media that he saw the emotionally charged chant "as an appeal to racial pride." Those cries, he felt, were a reflection of black frustration with the progress of civil rights.

Soon that cry became a belligerent shout of defiance, and with the younger generation of African-Americans growing impatient, King later saw it as a threat to the nonviolent movement. Years later, Andy Young told me that King understood the anger of the young then and thought they were "misguided kids."

The influence of the Black Power militants, however, began changing the course of the Movement; the old days of peaceful marches, boycotts and sit-ins began fading.

Northern cities that had thought themselves secure from racial strife suddenly were erupting into a pattern of spontaneous violence. Deadly riots spread to many major cities and lay waste to entire blocks with arson and looting.

In Chicago, King had begun an open housing campaign on behalf of the SCLC. He led marches through neighborhoods, bringing crowds of leering whites into the streets to throw cans and beer bottles and attempt to attack the marchers. A heavy protective police guard walked between the whites and the marchers.

Back home, King told reporters, "I've been in many demonstrations, all across the South, but I can say that I have never—not even in Mississippi and Alabama—seen mobs as hostile and hate filled as I've seen in Chicago."

The summer's violence and the black power movement brought the civil rights movement to a critical crossroads. A tragic impasse was in the making, an impasse in which blacks rioted because whites did not do enough and whites did not do enough because blacks rioted.

24

ATLANTA TAKES OFF

ATLANTA WAS A TREMENDOUSLY exciting city in the 1960s. The face of the city was going through vigorous change—its new skyline dominated by buildings that had mushroomed up.

Despite developing problems with race, Atlanta had begun the decade with unbridled expansion—steel girders raced each other up, rearing an even newer skyline all at once.

A young developer, John Portman, began the downtown transformation when he built the 23-story Merchandise Mart, the first of five skyscrapers on Peachtree Street.

Among them was the Regency Hyatt Hotel, designed by Portman. It dazzled Atlantans with its indoor atrium, the rooms opening onto balconies that overlooked the lobby.

On top of the hotel was the Polaris Lounge, a revolving bar made of dark blue glass in the shape of a flying saucer.

In those years, America was enthralled with space—astronauts were blasting off from Cape Canaveral.

Atlantans got into the act when a bank was built in the shape of a flying saucer and a filling station in the shape of a satellite.

Atlanta could not have risen as the foremost metropolis of the South without hard work and forward thinking of its leaders, black and white, who had the ability to negotiate.

William Hartsfield, who served six terms as mayor, is credited with developing Atlanta's airport into a national center, and also dubbed Atlanta as "the city too busy to hate."

Later, its white power structure was led by philanthropist Robert W. Woodruff, head of Coca-Cola. Woodruff gave close attention to efforts to enlarge and maintain the city's image and donated millions to the causes of the arts, education and health.

Ivan Allen Jr., a business and civic leader elected mayor, was the first to point out problems of race and schools. During his crusading leadership during the civil rights years, Atlanta served as a model for America's cities.

The Atlanta Journal and The Atlanta Constitution early on covered few racial stories. However, the editor of the Constitution, Ralph McGill, became nationally known for his daily columns, often against segregation.

Black leaders included Dr. King, his father, King Sr., Andy Young, Rev. Ralph Abernathy, Dr. Benjamin Mays and many others equally bent on solving its racial problems. They often met at Paschal's, a black-owned restaurant well-known for its power lunches. There, King and his aides brainstormed their next nonviolent assault on segregation and were sometimes joined by a few students and professors from Atlanta's black colleges and universities.

Lawyers, judges and clergymen in Atlanta also pushed hard against segregation. Catholic Archbishop Paul Hallinan ordered Catholic schools in his diocese integrated.

I had interviewed Hallinan before he was named archbishop. A native of Ohio, he told me he was impressed with Southerners' "love of their church and religion." After Hallinan read my story in a newspaper, he phoned to say he liked what I'd written but wished I had not referred to him as a "green-eyed cleric."

Donald Hollowell, a black lawyer who handled cases with consummate professionalism, helped integrate the University of Georgia, free King from prison and won a case requiring Atlanta's huge public hospital, Grady Memorial, to admit black doctors and dentists to its staff.

Elbert Tuttle, a great jurist, was the senior judge on the Fifth Circuit Court of Appeals, which ranged from the coast of Georgia to Texas. Tuttle was one of its courageous judges who used the law to fight for social justice and made a profound impact against racial discrimination.

Once, at a hearing before the tall, blue-eyed, white-haired Tuttle, so many spectators from SCLC and SNCC had come that it wasn't possible to seat them all. The solemn, dignified Tuttle surprised us by ordering that everyone be allowed in. They poured through the open doors, even sitting directly underneath the judge's bench and spilling into the corridors, where they sat on the floor.

In 1966, Julian Bond, a polished young man from a prominent black Atlanta family, won a seat in the Georgia House. He then committed an audacious act that won him instant celebrity. He burned his draft card in protest of the Vietnam War and, in retaliation, the House refused to allow him to take his seat. Bond appealed but had to wait two years before the U.S. Supreme Court overruled the legislature.

For relaxation during those fractious years, I sometimes went with a date to a darkened little cabaret theater called Wit's End, which featured a bright satirical revue that lampooned the Southern way of life. And Southern audiences, which by then included a few blacks, went for it.

"I see where one of the boys has been selected by Time magazine as man of the year," said a politician in one skit, referring to Dr. Martin Luther King Jr.

"And what have you done to honor him?" asked a reporter.

"Well," replied the politician, "we've decided to let

him register to vote." And though some of the barbs cast at racial prejudice were a bit biting, the clamorous applause from desegregated audiences proved they liked it.

When the owner of a bar went to court to force the 71 similar places in Atlanta to close down under Georgia's dry laws, the crisis was dealt with in a skit at Wit's End with "Gone With the Wind" characters.

"Miss Scarlett, Miss Scarlett," cried the little girl. "The Yankees are coming! The Yankees are coming!"

"Relax, Prissy," said Miss Scarlett. "Nobody's coming to Atlanta if they get rid of the liquor stores."

Wit's End proved Atlantans, black and white, could laugh at themselves. Satire, strong and sharp, kept customers coming back.

Atlantans, who had begun to feel they were solving racial concerns that Mayor Ivan Allen had warned about, suddenly found their mayor in the midst of a race riot.

The riot began after a policeman shot and wounded an auto thief during a race through the black section of Summerville. Hoping to quell the rock-throwing crowd, Mayor Allen, whose shining white hair stood out in the crowd, walked among them pleading, "Everybody go home, please."

At dusk, amid shouts and rocks flying around, Allen climbed on top a police car and, holding up a bullhorn, tried to speak through it. To the shock of the news media and those watching TV, the jeering crowd shoved the car, shaking the mayor to the ground.

Police dashed over, hustled Allen into a police car and sped away. One of the stones hit a TV reporter in the forehead, critically injuring him. Soon, Stokely Carmichael was weaving through city streets in a truck, shouting, "Black power," over a loudspeaker.

The incident angered many whites and a backlash came a week later, when segregationist Lester Maddox came in second in the Democratic primary for governor of Georgia. Later, after a runoff election, Maddox would become governor.

25

THE REVOLUTIONARY

CLAD IN A NEAT, dark suit and sitting comfortably in a swivel chair in his office with its dingy green walls and bare floors, Martin Luther King didn't seem like the revolutionary leader he was.

I had no idea that this would be my last interview with him—it was in 1968, not long before he was assassinated.

King had begun speaking of President Johnson's Great Society—the president's lifelong dream to revitalize our big cities, protect natural resources and guarantee educational opportunities for all.

But that great hope, King told me, was being shot down in the rice paddies of Vietnam. "A few years ago was a shining moment in the civil rights struggle," he said. "Then came the buildup in Vietnam and I watched the program broken as if it were an idle plaything of a society gone mad with war."

The nation's focus was on the war, and King's fierce distaste for it kept recurring. "The war must be stopped," he said. Already, he had urged every young man who finds the war "objectionable and unjust" to file as a conscientious objector.

Not only was King an eloquent speaker but he was a superb listener. At this point, he asked me, "How do you feel about U.S. involvement in Vietnam?" I was flattered that he'd ask my opinion.

King told me he would continue the struggle for equality that had begun in the black churches of the South, but now he had concluded that racism was only part of the problem—that poverty and the Vietnam War were major parts of it.

King's outspoken opposition to the war was raising fears among civil rights leaders of a stiffening white reaction. Some felt it was a mistake to put the issues of fighting for civil rights together with opposition to the war.

"We'll build our shanties—literal broken-down shanties—to dramatize and symbolize the day-to-day conditions for the way millions of people have to live," King said. The shanties were part of his strategy for a new-style massive demonstration of militant nonviolence.

At this time, King and the SCLC had begun organizing a coalition of black people, Hispanics and poor whites for the Poor People's Campaign.

His plan was to deal with the whole question of economic justice by taking this squatter army of the nation's poor to the Mall in Washington. There, the tumble-down shanties would contrast with the cherry blossoms along the Potomac.

I never doubted that King could draw thousands for that campaign. By promising "We shall overcome," he could keep on rousing them to face clubs, tear gas, fire hoses and attack dogs.

King's plans were not only to "house the troops of hopeless and embittered poor" he would lead to the capital, but also to dramatize the pain and suffering under which the hardscrabble poor lived at home.

His words reminded me of something he had said in an earlier speech: "Now we are a poor people. Don't let anybody fool you, we're poor. The vast majority of black people in the United States are smothering in an airtight cage of poverty in the midst of an affluent society...."

King then spoke of the alternative to nonviolence, which he never tired of repeating: "I've been to the ghettos; I know the resentments will blow up if something is not done quickly. We're going all out to get this nation to respond to nonviolence. If it refuses to do this, it will entitle the Negro to so intensify his anger that we will go deeper and deeper into chaos."

While violence created outrage, televised accounts of such events also dramatized the injustice facing his people. King used that strategy in an effort to "shame the nation into action."

When he told me the army of protesters in the

Poor People's Campaign was to invade "the very seat of power," I asked, "How effective would they be?"

He replied that he had few illusions about persuading Congress to action. "Congress sits there, recalcitrant, a sickness upon them. When you look at Congress, you see they are never moved to act unless the nation gets them to move. We never got the civil rights bill until we had Selma. A new kind of Selma is needed," he said.

King told me he had long weighed and agonized over the risk of such action, but he felt the Poor People's campaign was a "last-ditch chance for nonviolence."

I asked, "What about the risk of a takeover by extremists?"

King replied, "I am convinced I can control them. If we came to a situation where our actions were leading to violence, I would call it off."

He began talking about the enormous wealth of America, which he felt should be used through tax policies to promote chances of a decent life for the poor. Already, King had called for a guaranteed annual wage—a call that alarmed not only the business world, but the federal government.

Some black leaders and scholars thought King's plans for his Poor People's Campaign were becoming too militant, and a few were beginning to desert him, saying he should stick to civil rights.

King also spoke of the pressures facing him,

including criticism from his own staff. There were times when he had to oppose his own followers, when he felt it necessary to take his message to a wider public.

At this time, King was either admired or hated. Among his followers he was known as "the Leader," "Moses," and at SCLC, "Mr. President."

King was an ordained Baptist minister, a graduate of Morehouse College and of Crozer Theological Seminary in Pennsylvania, with a doctorate in theology from Boston University. It always seemed shocking to me to hear him derisively called, even by blacks, "de Lawd," "Kingfish" and "Martin Luther Coon."

As a symbol of integration, he was the object of unrelenting, sometimes brutal attacks. As these increased, King steadily became overworked, and I noticed how tired he was beginning to look.

With his guiding principle of nonviolent action, King became the symbol of the black struggle. Their revolt against more than a century of oppression could easily have gone in a different, even deadly direction. It did not, thanks to King's creed of nonviolence.

More than any other man, King was the voice of the Movement. Yet, in the heyday of the '60s, a great many others helped change America. Too little credit is given to the women who were crucial in the fight to end segregation, as were the many capable young black ministers who worked with King.

After King was killed, two of his trusted friends,

Harry Belafonte, the singer and activist, and Stanley Levison, a white lawyer and longtime adviser to King, wrote, "Under his leadership millions of black Americans emerged from spiritual imprisonment, from fear, from apathy, and took to the streets to proclaim their freedom."

Those words echoed what King himself once said: "The real victory was what this period did to the psyche of the black man. The greatness of this period was that we armed ourselves with dignity and self-respect."

After his death, some whites—and a few blacks—tried to transform him into merely a dreamer. King was a dreamer, all right, but he was also a revolutionary who led his people in a powerful revolt, and by 1965, the Jim Crow law of segregation was legally dead.

26

CORETTA'S LAST YEARS

Only days after burying her husband, Coretta King began to take up his work—as she had promised the congregation at Ebenezer Church on Easter morning.

She began planning the Martin Luther King Jr. Center for Nonviolent Change, working first from her home. She called, asking if I'd bring in as many newspaper stories about King as I could. I dug through piles of newspapers filled with stories of his life and death that were coming daily to our office. I also carried dozens to her home, lugging them out of my car onto her porch.

Coretta later set up office in the basement of an Atlanta University Center building. Although she was refusing all interviews at that time, I sometimes dropped by to chat and ask how her work was advancing.

A year after King's death, I asked, "Coretta, do you think you'd ever consider marrying again? You're young and you'll surely have plenty of chances."

"Oh," she replied, throwing her head back and laughing, "I'd have to think about that!" Then she added somberly, "No, I don't think so."

Coretta struggled to pay bills and rear her four children, supporting the family by fees she was beginning to earn from speeches. I was at her home when Marty, her eldest son, came in and told her he wanted to run for a Fulton County commissioner's seat, but would need $5,000 to register. "Where am I going to get $5,000!" Coretta exclaimed. Marty did register and won the election.

She devoted her life to continuing her husband's legacy, working tirelessly to develop the King Center and establish his birthday as a national holiday.

I always found Coretta to be a warm, caring person, confident in her own actions, who became a legend in her own right, speaking out for women's rights, economic issues and world peace.

Thirty years after King was killed, she was still living in their home on Sunset Avenue, but the neighborhood had declined and the house had been burglarized. Television star Oprah Winfrey bought new digs for Coretta at Park Place, an expensive Buckhead high-rise with beautiful rooms and a panoramic view of downtown Atlanta. Several years later, Coretta suffered a stroke, then another more debilitating stroke.

Following her children's wishes, she visited a specialist in California and holistic doctors in Mexico, where she died on Jan. 30, 2006.

Coretta touched the lives of several generations, and her funeral was attended by then President George

W. Bush and three past presidents, George H. W. Bush, Bill Clinton and Jimmy Carter.

I'd parked at the Atlanta Civic Center and walked to one of the many buses waiting to take people to the church. I was told to board a certain bus and was surprised to find it filling with family friends of the Kings, members of the Atlanta City Council and mayor's office.

We were escorted by motorcade to the New Birth Missionary Baptist Church in Lithonia, Georgia, where, before police allowed us out, the bus next to us unloaded the presidential group and members of Congress.

The politicians walked into the church first. Then, our group, packed tightly together in the long hallway, was held up more than an hour and a half until King family members were in their seats. Finally, we filed in behind them. I wasn't happy about where I was sitting, since I could see Coretta's face in her coffin, directly in front, several rows down, during six hours of eulogies. It was upsetting.

During the six-hour service, there were frequent outbursts of approval from the audience: "Amen! Amen!" or "Yes! Yes!" in reaction to a speaker.

A well-known Atlanta black activist, the Rev. Joseph Lowery, chided President Bush, who was sitting behind him on the podium. Lowery told the audience, "We know now there were no weapons of mass destruction [in Iraq]. But Coretta knew, and we knew, there were weapons of misdirection right down here. Millions without health insurance, poverty abounds. For war, billions more, but no more for the poor."

Lowery's criticism of President Bush about the U.S. war in Iraq brought much laughter from the audience but seemed disrespectful to many, under the circumstances.

Bernice, the youngest of King's children, was also an ordained minister and delivered her mother's eulogy in a voice with power and cadence that echoed her father's.

After the services, we had to wait again for the honored guests to leave, then for the coffin to be carried out. Dusk was settling on Atlanta as our bus arrived at the King Center, where the street was roped off for a private burial. On the other side of the rope, hundreds of folks were peering over, trying to see what they could.

Coretta's coffin was placed on the grass in a small area shadowed by trees and bushes, next to Ebenezer Church. Her children released white doves that flew around the church and lit in the tall, dark trees above us. Bouquets of red roses decorated the wall along the sidewalk, and the brief ceremony, with a few prayers and songs, was both moving and fitting.

Then we were driven back to the Civic Center, where I got my car and drove to the Omni Hotel with my invitation for the family dinner. Guests included some 100 people, and I seemed to be one of the very few whites present. Tables were set with plates and silverware and we helped ourselves at a long table laden with roast beef, chicken, potatoes, various salads and delicious desserts.

I sat with friends of Coretta's family, who'd driven from Marion, Alabama, and after dinner, I walked over to speak with the King children. Marty wasn't there, but Yoki and Dexter stood up and hugged me. I shook hands with Bernice and introduced myself—she did not remember me.

A few years later, at the ceremony releasing "Desert Rose," a book about her mother's life, we chatted and I found Bernice, who had graduated from Spelman College and Emory Law School, to be an intelligent, delightful young woman.

EPILOGUE

"Aunt Kathryn, how come you can't be normal like other people's aunts?" asked my young niece Becky as I switched the TV program the three children were watching to a news broadcast of a racial demonstration in the South.

While vacationing at my sister's home, I needed to keep up with fast-breaking news events. But the child's unexpected question made me realize how much my work differed from the usual woman-friendly jobs of the '60s.

"What would you like me to be?" I asked.

"Oh," she said, "a secretary or a teacher."

The child had heard me describing events I'd been covering to my sister and brother-in-law. She imagined an aunt whose life was "more normal," not one consumed with interest in racial happenings. My life was often chaotic, pressured, fascinating—and anything but normal.

The South was at war over civil rights, and agonizing conflict over American commitment in Vietnam was dividing the country. At the same time, we were jammed with breaking news and shocking tragedy—our president had been assassinated, and America's greatest civil rights leader shot to death by a sniper.

I was reluctant even to take a vacation, afraid I'd miss out on some significant event. But after all the extra hours I'd worked covering King's funeral in April 1968 and wanting to see my young nieces and nephew, I took a week off in June. My sister, Rita, and her family were living in Puerto Rico because my brother-in-law, George Besbekos, was then stationed at the U.S. Navy base at Roosevelt Roads. I'd gone swimming in the nearby ocean and came back to the house to watch the California presidential primary in Los Angeles on television.

Suddenly, breaking news came—Democratic presidential candidate Bobby Kennedy had been fatally shot. Only two months earlier, I'd seen Kennedy walking out of Ebenezer Church at King's funeral. In those years, almost every week brought unbelievable news.

Still, the challenge and excitement of those years was incredible. Each assignment was an adventure into uncharted waters. I loved my work and minded neither the overload nor the variety of assignments. When you're involved in a hot story, your brain is always absorbed, thinking about it, and having endless energy, I thrived on the pressure.

Even now, all these years later, I feel a strong sense of privilege at having known the Kings and played a part in telling their remarkable story.

APPENDIXES

APPENDIX A

KATHRYN JOHNSON: AN ORAL HISTORY

March 21, 2007

The Associated Press Oral History Program
Interview by VALERIE S. KOMOR, *Director, AP Corporate Archives*
with MARY MURPHY, *independent film & television writer/producer*
[*transcript edited for length*]

[*Tape one*]

KOMOR: Good morning.

JOHNSON: Morning.

KOMOR: I'm Valerie Komor, and I'm interviewing today for the Oral History Project of the AP Corporate Archives, Kathryn Johnson. And, thank you for being here, Kathryn.

JOHNSON: You're welcome.

KOMOR: Today is March 21st, is it? Of 2007. Kathryn, let's start at the beginning. Where were you born, and when were you born, and tell us about your family.

JOHNSON: OK. I was born in the Deep South,

Columbus, Georgia, which is right on the banks of the Chattahoochee River; separates Georgia from Alabama, and I was born in 1926. I have two siblings, and I grew up along the Chattahoochee playing on the river at a time when women—when children could play unmolested, totally, up and down the river. And, I had a wonderful childhood, and, I grew up when—well, I went to Agnes Scott College. You want to get into that now?

KOMOR: I'd love to.

JOHNSON: And, I wa—I was accepted at two different colleges, but, out of state, but Mother wanted me to be a little closer to home, that was about a two-hour drive, that's in Decatur, Georgia, right on the suburb of Atlanta. And, it was a bluestocking sort of a school, and the reason I went there was because my father was dying, and World War II was raging. World War II was underway when I entered Agnes Scott.

KOMOR: What year did you enter?

JOHNSON: I entered in '43.

KOMOR: And did you know what you wanted to study at that point?

JOHNSON: I majored in English, and I didn't study journalism. I love to read because my mother read to us at night to put us to sleep almost every night, and I loved writing, and I loved reading, you know, reading. But there was no journalism major there, and so I majored in English. And when I graduated, I knew I wanted to write, but in those years, a woman had a choice of being a nurse or a teacher or a librarian or to get married later, but—and that was it. And so I went into night school at Georgia State, but I went to The Associated Press, and they—there were no women then, there had been, I think, one...

KOMOR: Where was the office? Which AP office is this?

JOHNSON: The Atlanta office.

KOMOR: I see.

JOHNSON: Yes, right after I graduated from Agnes Scott.

KOMOR: Did you move, yourself, to Atlanta?

JOHNSON: I just stayed on. Mother moved, later on, to Atlanta.

KOMOR: I see. So...

JOHNSON: Because my sister also graduated from another college in Georgia and she wanted to live in Atlanta. So, that's how I ended up there after graduation.

KOMOR: So you called up the AP office?

JOHNSON: I did, and I went by, and I wanted to write—to be a writer, and they were sort of stunned, because I think they had had one woman as a radio writer years earlier, and there were no women in the Atlanta bureau, and they weren't wanted; definitely not wanted {laughs}. But he told me I could be a secretary and work my way into it.

KOMOR: And who is 'he'? Who was the bureau chief?

JOHNSON: W. F. Caldwell, and he was about to

retire. But he respected the fact that I had graduated and loved to write, and he let me write features, which got printed on the wires, occasionally. And, so I applied to The American Newspaper Guild, and they said that I could—should get on, and meanwhile, I went to Georgia State and took journalism. And, I...

KOMOR: Was the war over at this point?

JOHNSON: No. The war ended as sophomores.

KOMOR: OK.

JOHNSON: And we, we, it was fascinating, we used to smash cans to help the war effort, and so forth. Well, when you get involved in college life, you, you know, forget it. My older brother was only about 18 or 19, and he was in the Pacific fighting, and I had two young uncles, and one of them was—his ship was sunk at Okinawa, so the war was very much with us, you know, at that time. But it—when I got into, into the Guild, I had worked at—well, I was still working as a secretary, and meanwhile, I got engaged, so I wasn't very anxious to, to go ahead with AP. But, he was killed.

KOMOR: Oh, I'm sorry.

JOHNSON: So, I just threw myself into my work. And by that time, the Guild insisted that they try me out. And meanwhile, I had taken a course that—a journalism course from Don Carter, who was the city editor, head foreman, and city editor of the Atlanta Journal, and he took my exam, which was 500 questions about what is the good news, and what isn't, and I got 495 right. And The AP still insisted I try out again for three more months, {laughs} on probation. I knew I wasn't wanted, but anyway, they, they were forced to accept me, finally. And by the end, Wes Gallagher, I think, was the general editor, general...

KOMOR: General manager, yes.

MURPHY: Kathryn, do you remember any of those questions?

JOHNSON: Any of those news questions?

MURPHY: I mean, yeah, yeah.

JOHNSON: The 495? Oh, they was just sort of normal ones, you know, if—what should be on the front page, this, you know, that kind of thing, that's about all I remember, but it was part of the course. He, he took it because he was rather pleased, and he thought that would really force my boss to take me, but it didn't. So when I got on, I, I didn't care, I was delighted, and I didn't even regard myself as a woman, I just was a news—newsperson. And, I mean, not trying to push—there was none of the feminism that you have today. And most of the guys I knew, they, particularly the young ones, didn't want me, but the older ones were pros, and they taught me. In, in those years, Atlanta accepted about one person a year, and trained them thoroughly.

And I was beautifully trained by the, by the Atlanta people.

KOMOR: Who were some of your mentors in Atlanta?

JOHNSON: Well, I, I really didn't have any {laughs} mentors.

KOMOR: Well, who were these people you're referring to, who were so helpful to you?

JOHNSON: Well, well, one of them was the night editor, and they [were] in charge of teaching young people. And he had a ruler, I'll never forget it, I was sitting across from him on the desk, {laughs} and he'd ask me questions about a story I was writing, and if I didn't answer correctly, he'd tap me on the knuckles with a ruler. {Laughs} That was really like being back in school.

KOMOR: My word.

JOHNSON: Not badly, I mean, but you know, it was—that's how I got the civil rights movement, because I was young and green and cheap labor [...] and the men didn't want it.

KOMOR: Why do you suppose that was?

JOHNSON: Because, I think, they were—most of them were very lovely guys. They're not—they weren't racist in the sense that they are today, in many ways, they weren't Klansmen types, but they did not want to cover a black movement. And, so when I got it—but when Martin Luther King [Jr.] became famous, they wanted it then.

KOMOR: I see.

JOHNSON: And, but then I had it sewed up. I, I had all the access....

KOMOR: Yes.

JOHNSON: To the Kings, and to Andy Young, and John Lewis.

KOMOR: How did that start, your relationship with the Kings [unintelligible]?

JOHNSON: Well, my first assignment I got, I think, was at the—called the Link Club, which was a rather exclusive black club for, for black professionals, and there were quite a few doctors, and lawyers, and they were lovely people, and perfectly well educated. It was astonishing to me, too, because I was a Southern girl brought up in Columbus, I had known blacks only as—we had a nurse because there were three little ones Mother had, and then we had a yardman, and a one-day-a-week maid, and that's my only experience. And I could, you know, I saw the shotgun houses that they lived in but I was totally unaware of the humiliation, and the racism, and the poverty that, that was now being exposed to me as a reporter, you know. And the Link Club was probably the most—the first opening, and then I went to some little...

KOMOR: Did you write a story about it?

JOHNSON: I wrote a story about it, yes. And, that was the first taste I had of—they were mostly very light colored, and I thought that was interesting, too, you know, that they were—had gotten so far ahead, in a sense. And I had—I was just totally unaware of, of...

KOMOR: I see. And this was the late '50s? The beginning...

JOHNSON: It started out in '59.

KOMOR: '59.

JOHNSON: And, and '60, '61...

[*interruption*]

KOMOR: And—but when did you first meet Martin Luther King?

JOHNSON: [...] I got—I guess my first—I, I had seen him and covered him at news conferences, and so forth, but it was the Scripto march was really the first time I had—they had—there was a strike at Scripto, which was a manufacturing plant near downtown Atlanta, and it was late at night and freezing cold and I could tell I was the only reporter there but I had been called to go, and, The AP knew that I would go to cov—cover these things, because I found it fascinating, you know—it was a life-transforming experience for me, the civil rights movement was, and by then I went on my own, and covered him on thi—on this particular strike, and I asked him questions about, you know, "Why the strike?" The usual questions, and, "You want higher pay," and whatnot. And I looked around, and there was just one TV group there, and they were covering him, but there [I] was [the] only white person that I could see around there. So when it was over at about 11 o'clock, King had been marching, and he told me, and I was freezing to death, I had a coat up, and he said, "It's a dangerous section of town, and I want you to let me—and walk you to your car." So he did, and it was a couple of blocks away. And it was so cold, I said, "Well, let me take you home," because I knew then he lived not too far away near the, you know, universities and so I took him, I drove him home, and Coretta [King] met us at the door, and she was—and she came out to the car, and told me to come in for coffee, I knew Coretta, too. [...]

KOMOR: So would it be fair to say, Kathryn, that he was a great inspiration to your own coverage of the movement?

JOHNSON: Yes, he was. He definitely was. That, and discovering—and talking to so many young blacks, and what they were doing. When they integrated the Crystal, for example, I was sent, and...

KOMOR: What was the Crystal?

JOHNSON: It's a small, little café that serves little hamburgers and coffee, and it was downtown Atlanta, and not too far from AP. So, I stood in the back, and the white countermen poured hot grits over the young black students' heads, and they had been trained to nonviolence, then. That was going on considerably in the late '50s and early '60s. And I think this was '61. It was not long after the integration at, you know, North Carolina, the Woolworth's. And I watched the grits fall down their heads, and they sat there and took it, and, you know, it aroused my sense of humanity and justice and I began really having, you know, that's one reason I was able to put—give so much of my own time to cov— to the coverage, because every time I'd call my boss and say I need this—this is going on, and so forth, and I—because I—they—I would get a call, and he would say, "We can't afford it. The budget is blown." And I'm sure it was, because it—there were demonstrations against the Vietnam War, then, as well as civil rights going on in the '60s, and our budget was always blown.

[*interruption*]

KOMOR: Did you have a role in the Kennedy assassination coverage at all?

JOHNSON: Kennedy assassination? No, no. I was sent on a plane, I was flying to Dallas. I got the ticket and I was supposed to go to Dallas and then we got word that he had died so, that all stopped all that. No, I didn't. But I saw Jackie Kennedy a couple of times, you remember, at the King house and so forth.

KOMOR: Yes. Yes. Describe, describe your relationship with, with the Kings and how it evolved over the years, and when you were able to cover Coretta following the death of her husband.

JOHNSON: Yeah. Well, I had been writing about Coretta and—off and on—because she sang a great deal, you know, and she had a wonderful voice; she was trained to sing, and she would call me about—and tell me some things that were going on and I would get involved with her. I knew she loved music and she knew I had a passion for opera and she'd call me when Leontyne Price, was the first black to integrate the opera in Atlanta, and, she was going to sing and she'd call me at work and say that she could not get tickets but Martin Luther King was her husband who's going to be in town that week and that they wanted to go. And so I called the opera and said, "Look, these people now are famous and I would think you had—" I know they saved tickets at the end and said, "No way," they had none. So I gave them my two, to Coretta.

But that was the first time that a black was singing in Atlanta in the opera. So it was big news and so I was able to use my press pass to get in to listen to it myself. And Leontyne Price, somehow, I don't know how she got word that the Kings were there and she invited them backstage to meet her after the opera. They were very thrilled and I had a phone call and Coretta passed me on to Dr. King and they thanked me for the tickets. So, we just, off and on.

KOMOR: You talked about your experience covering civil rights and covering King as self-transforming. Would you talk a little bit more about that, what you mean by that?

JOHNSON: Well, as a child, you know, I grew up in a very segregated society. Everything was black and white, even for water fountains and even the entrance to the courthouse, you know, they had to go through the black entrance. And when I grew up, as I said, we had a nurse whom we loved dearly and we had a yardman and we played with his two children, he would bring twin sons when they were growing up, when we were all very young, but I did not know any other blacks except, you know, as servants and I had never realized, Dr. King really was so brilliant, that was just transforming to realize that the way they lived in such poverty and degradation, really, and I felt—my sense of justice and humanity was really aroused and it was aroused by covering the movement. And I think it was just a fluke that I got the movement but I think it was, you know, it was transforming. And I thought, when I was growing up, that—it never occurred to me that that was wrong, segregation, it was just the way it was until I got into the covering the movement. You know, even Coretta King coming back from the famous speech "I Have a Dream," they stopped at a, she told me, they stopped at a filling station, she wanted to go to the ladies' room and it was only for whites, they wouldn't let her. This was in Virginia, coming back down, driving back down to Atlanta. But it really—it was only until I got into covering the civil rights movement that, that I really changed completely.

[*Tape two*]

MURPHY: Getting back to Martin Luther King, for one second, you know, there are a zillion books that we've all read now, and the portrayal of him is as a very, you know, a human but flawed individual. Did you have a sense of any of those flaws?

JOHNSON: Any of those what, now?

MURPHY: Flaws. That—Martin Luther King, despite the brilliance that you talk about...

JOHNSON: Oh, the flaws, yeah.

MURPHY: Flawed.

JOHNSON: Well, you know, the womanizing and so forth you're talking about.

[*interruption*]

JOHNSON: I heard all of that. I heard rumors galore and I believe it, because I heard too much from too many people who really were in the know. And—but I never saw it personally, OK? You know, I didn't. But I've had a number of black friends who have talked about it, and that was a really serious flaw, I think, but it had nothing to do with his ability as a great leader, I don't think. I'm writing a book and I'm not putting any of that in there because I didn't see it, frankly. And, anyway, he was late, he was always late for meetings—he was always pushed—busy and so forth, and we were—he would say this is CPT, which meant "colored people time." And I wouldn't forget when I was in Washington covering a talk from a member of Congress and they were—I was sitting at a table with a bunch of reporters, mostly Washington Post and New York Times and they were having Jesse Jackson come and when Jesse was late, and he was very late, nobody was ever late at that meeting, and this was about—half hour he was late and I said, finally, "I guess maybe a CPT." And they looked at me and I said, "That's colored people time."

And I didn't mean—that's what King said at himself, you know, in the South, and so, boy, the movement away from me was so obvious {laughs}. And then when Jesse came, he looked around and he didn't know any—and he spotted me and he came straight to me and I stood up to greet him and he hugged me and kissed me on both cheeks, which really startled them because I sounded, I guess I sounded, racist, you know, that was funny. King—I think Coretta, Coretta ignored all of that. We never talked about it, we're fairly good friends, particularly after King died, she started up a little office in the basement of one of the black universities in Atlanta and I—she wanted newspapers about his death and I brought in dozens and dozens from The AP and we sat there and talked and all and—but she had—she felt that he had done great things as a nonviolent and he had and that's what she was determined to do. But—so I really never, I never saw that, personally. But then I was always just on hard news reporting, so I wouldn't.

KOMOR: Now how did your friendship with Coretta develop after Martin's death?

JOHNSON: Well, it developed, probably, even more because she wanted me to talk to her and so forth and I'd go down to the university and then we would have lunch and have, you know, so forth. [...] Mainly she wanted to talk about what she was doing and, you know, to advance her husband and she did, greatly, I think. And one thing she was doing was to have a—she and

Daddy King both were at Ebenezer Church on January 15th, on his birthday, and it began very slowly the first years because it was just, you know, Ebenezer people never invited—few reporters, but after that, of course, it got bigger and bigger and parades and so forth. But early on, I had gone every time and sat on the front row in order to cover—listen to the people talking and I'd go early and I knew the janitor, now maintenance man, at Ebenezer, and he would always let me in early, and I'd go in and find a seat and put my pocketbook and my briefcase and so forth down on the floor and then walk around talking to different people in the congregation and I'll never forget how I felt about the congregation at Ebenezer. You could see these people there with such fervor and they were beaten down and they were—lived in poverty and were worn out, but they never lost their faith and they were—they had a great will to survive and they were doing it, and so I really felt strongly about, you know, helping on that score then and helping Coretta. I didn't think it would ever get to the point that it got, but I went back to my seat and somebody—there was a man who was sitting in my seat had taken all my things out of my seat and put it on the floor. So I said, "I'm sorry, I came early to get that seat." And he said, "I'm from—with TV and I'm from New York." {Laughs} So, anyway, as we stood arguing, I heard this voice booming out and, Daddy King, and Daddy King was a powerful old patriarch and he saw, he saw that we were arguing, and he motioned with me, you know, "Come over here." I—the King family was sitting on the second row and first row and so forth and, so I picked up my things and—you didn't disobey Daddy King, I mean, he was—and I went and Coretta and the children moved over and I sat between Coretta and Daddy King for the—but I was still miffed because on the front row, you know, you could see; right? But, I just had that sort of a very, very fond relationship and I suppose it comes from—it came—they recognized that I'd been doing, I think, a lot extra. And, I went on a lot of dusty marches that had been set up that King was on for a while and Andy Young would move and everybody would be hot and dirty and Andy would be there with his fresh, white shirt—he could always look so crisp.

KOMOR: Would you tell us about the Selma march?

JOHNSON: The Selma march? Well, when I drove there with another AP guy and there's, there were signs along the way as we got outside of Selma saying, "King was a communist," because he'd gone to that particular school that had some communist sympathy—he was not a communist, but we got outside of Selma, and it was a very small group being formed and I settled in a motel and went to the march, and at the beginning it was just so—you wouldn't believe it, I mean, just a few hundred people. There were a few white people and a few girls that, I was a little surprised, they were barefooted {laughs} march—real strong advocates of the civil rights, you know, but—and the helicopters were going up over us like hummingbirds, you know, just—and so we started out that way, but it—I'll be honest, I did not sleep out in the fields because it was messy and muddy, it was—been raining a few days, and I always hitched a ride back to Montgomery and spent the, I mean, to Selma and got—and stayed in the—no, it was Montgomery—and went back to Montgomery, yeah, and then we'd get a ride back and march for hours and hours. But then I had stories to file. We had people all along the route, you know, and it—towards the end, King had not been with us for two or three days and then he'd come towards the end, 'cause he had had other commitments. It's been such a long time, I didn't—hadn't thought too much about that, because there'd been so much written, but—toward the end there—many celebrities came and played music and sang for us and that kind of thing and it revived the march tremendously. By the time that we—everybody marched into Montgomery, it was about 25,000 people and, King gave us a wonderful, wonderful talk on the steps of the capitol, which Montgomery was the cradle of the Confederacy, you know, when Jefferson Davis was the president, that was the Confederacy. So that was kind of a very meaningful thing. [...] Incredible events, you know, and, the '60s was a—one of the most violent decades I think in the history of this country with the exception maybe of the civil rights, I mean, Civil War and the Revolution, because, you know, a president, U.S. president was assassinated, a presidential candidate—well, another president resigned, Nixon did, and another presidential candidate, Kennedy, was, was shot to death and America's leading civil rights leader was, Martin Luther King, was assassinated, so it was just one violent thing after the other.

[*interruption*]

KOMOR: Of course the other huge story going on at the same time as the civil rights movement was Vietnam, and you played a central role in that story when you covered the Calley trial. Would you talk to us about that, Kathryn? How did that story come to you?

JOHNSON: Lou Boccardi called down and told my—Autry then, that I should go to cover the Calley trial at Fort Benning. And, so I was called in and told that I didn't have to accept it if I didn't want to, because I knew that—I was scheduled to work desk tricks for the next few weeks and he would've had to fill them, I could understand he had a problem, you know, and then—but I didn't have to because it would be a lot of hard work and so on. But I told him I would—I wanted to go.

KOMOR: Why did you want to go?

JOHNSON: Because I thought it would be interesting. I was very—I was really quite fearless. I look back and I think I attribute it to my childhood with my brother.

KOMOR: In what respect?

JOHNSON: Well, I had an older brother who was a rogue, {laughs} so to speak. A lovely guy, but, loved him dearly, but when we were very young, for example, the Chattahoochee River was very choppy then, they've, they closed it off sort of now, but at that time, you know, we were warned never, never ever swim in the—I tried to—you know, my father taught us to swim very early. I was 3 years old. I don't even remember learning, you know, but we were told you never go out on the river. Well, my brother, there was a bateau right next to the shore and it was leaking a little bit and he says, "Sis, let's play Huckleberry Finn." Well, this is my older brother and he was a lot of fun, I knew he was always—and so I—we got in the boat, I was about 5 or 6 years old, I vague—I remember it all right, but when we started floating down the Chattahoochee, the water started coming in and there were two older black fishermen, they were older men, because I remember they had gray hair and, they spotted us and they paddled over to us and grabbed—took us out of that bateau and took us into their boat and just as, about the time that was going underwater, and they took us to shore. And, when I was about 6 years old then, we were—my father was a hunter and he had guns, but they were all locked up in a big cabinet, I remember that, and the bullets were kept elsewhere and we were warned, you know, never, never to go in that, and we never did, but he had a friend whose father was also a hunter, and that boy got their father's .22 rifle and they put a can on my head and shot it off, and I would go and get the can and put it back, but fortunately they were excellent shots {laughs}. And Mother finally saw it and stopped it, of course, and she called my father to come home from work. And my father was one of these kind of guys who would—Mother was the disciplinarian, he would—but he took off that leather belt and he really lit into the—both boys and they were really shook, you know, 'cause I could've been killed, I mean—and I would do things that he wanted me to do that were terribly dangerous, but I didn't know any better then.

And I grew up that way, I mean, he dared me off of high dives and, and then I had two uncles, Mother's much younger brothers, Mother grew up in Savannah, Georgia, and they, they would play baseball with my brother, and they were older, they were late teens, but still they would play ball. I would follow them because they lived on one of the squares, it was beautiful, Savannah, you know, it's—on squares there, and they were at a baseball game on, I remember at the—Colonial Cemetery was right nearby and the Colonial Cemetery is—it—now kept up very well—the cement round it had whole families into them, these big, brick squares with the round cement tops, and some of the cement tops were broken off and the boys just took a piece off and put me inside. Of course there was nothing but ground if, you know, if—dirt, and then they put the top back on to—so I'd stay inside, they wouldn't lose me, and I would spend hours inside the tomb. {Laughs} And—delighted that the boys would let me follow them, you know, and I guess I was a tomboy, I never thought about it, but I guess. But a little sun would come through and I'd play with the little doodlebugs just to amuse myself. So I think, I think all that had a lot to do why I was not really too worried about these—some of the very dangerous situations that took place, you know, in Atlanta. [...] But, I'm sorry I digressed but—go back to [Lieutenant William L.] Calley.

KOMOR: Sure.

JOHNSON: I decided to drive down and, by myself, because—there were—Art Everett from New York and Harry Rosenthal from Washington...

KOMOR: Yeah.

JOHNSON: I think, yeah—were there and the three of us were covering the trial, and I drove down, it was, I remember it because it was a flaming autumn of red and gold trees were—beautiful driving into Fort Benning and of course I grew up in Columbus, which is right next to Fort Benning; I knew Fort Benning well. And, it was fascinating. It brought home the whole war, listening to the witnesses, to us, and all the brutality and the horror of Vietnam was there in the trial every day, you know, and...

KOMOR: How long did that trial last?

JOHNSON: Oh, that—it lasted from—four and a half months long, in the fall and it was, I think, March the 31st or something like 30th it ended.* And when it did end and I walked out front, I looked around and there were jonquils and azaleas that were—everything was beautiful and all in bloom, and I had been totally unaware of the passing seasons because the trial was just totally fascinating, you know.

KOMOR: And you went there every single day.

JOHNSON: Oh yeah. Well, the week—they usually stopped over the weekend, and they stopped at a certain time at night. Sometimes they would go late.

KOMOR: Would you set the scene in that courtroom for us?

JOHNSON: The what?

KOMOR: Will you please set the scene in that courtroom? If you can.

JOHNSON: There were, there were six officers, and they had—they all had served in, in, you know, World War II and so forth, I mean, they had great—that you—they were all colonels and majors and men had seen a great deal of service and so he was, he was really judged

* The Calley Trial began in November 17th, 1970, and sentencing was March 31st, 1971.

not only by his peers but a superior group, you know, and mostly they were—not a whole lot of outsiders, an awful lot of officers. I don't know whether it was restricted or not, but it was nothing like the Lemuel Penn trial and so forth, that anybody could go in and so forth. Calley, Calley really thought he—I got to know Calley well because I went every night with one of the photographers, either Joe Holloway or Charlie Kelly, they both were there off—one at a time, you know, and...

KOMOR: Yeah.

JOHNSON: And the first one I went to because a Life magazine man had invited Charlie to a cookout with Calley and he said, "Bring," you know, "that woman reporter." So I went and that's how I got to—began to know Calley. And he started inviting a group of photographers and reporters to his, to his little apartment every night and—to drink and...

KOMOR: During the trial?

JOHNSON: Oh yeah, during the trial, every night after the trial. And it was interesting in his apartment. It had a big sign, "No More War," you know, "No More," and it had a big flag there which somebody sent him saying that it was at the Battle of the Bulge and a veteran had given him and so forth. And he was, he was extremely down to earth, I think, honest, I think, I personally think, Calley should never have been accepted as an officer.

KOMOR: Why?

JOHNSON: I don't think he had the—I think he was intelligent, but he didn't have the background sufficient that I think was needed for an officer. But the Army, then, was scraping the bottom of the barrel because so many young people were going to Canada or going to college and they were able to get out of going, of going to Vietnam. So they had to get, had to get them. I just—and he had not heard of the Geneva Convention[s], you know, I thought he wasn't—he'd dropped out of high school but he finally had gone back and finished. His mother was dead and he would not allow his father or his two sisters, younger sisters, to come because he didn't want them to be, you know, embarrassed with the trial and so forth. But he had a girlfriend, a redhead girlfriend, who worked at Fort Benning, and they would have drinks there at night and, and it was, it was interesting to talk to, because then you were able to pick up little, little odds and ends, and I was able to get a feature out of it almost every day. And then New York came to depend on the features, now, I wasn't supposed to be doing features but, you know, it was interesting. And, for example, you know, he, he would kill a cockroach and he said, "It's like a body count in Vietnam, you counted the dead animals," and so forth, I mean, you know, just—that was sort of macabre humor, but it was well—it did well on feature stories, you know, because it was...

KOMOR: Color.

JOHNSON: Yeah.

KOMOR: Yeah.

JOHNSON: And, when—it became—he thought he would be freed; he really did. And they planned a big to-do and everything. And, and Art Everett would never come to the house, although I invited Art. But Art was getting a little old then, too, and he wanted to go home and call his wife and so forth. And, and Harry Rosenthal said, "I can't go because it's like going to Adolf Eichmann," covering Adolf Eichmann, and, so I understood that. And so I was the only one that went at night and, so, I really, I really did get to know him well. And two weeks that they debated on the—just short of two weeks on the verdict. And I felt that, I felt that most likely he would be convicted, just sort of, you know, got that way. You felt—we were assuming, I don't know, but, anyway, he didn't, he didn't. So I told him, I said, "What about—let me get an interview with you, two of them; one of them if you're convicted and the other is if you are freed." And I gave him my word I will only use one and it—"Whatever happens, I promise." And he trusted me and—with good reason, because on something like that, you know, and so I interviewed him, and it was just Joe Holloway there, and the AP book on Calley, the pictures of him smoking, he smoked all the time, that was during the interview. And I got the two of them. And I went back to my—the motel and typed them both up into, you know, stories, and I tucked them away inside my pocketbook. And so when, when he was convicted and taken away and told not to talk to a single reporter, you know, AP came out with a—the conviction thing I had and they were...

KOMOR: How did you, how did you—did you dash from the courtroom? And—how did you get the story out of the court-martial?

JOHNSON: Oh, well, oh yeah, oh yeah, I dashed down the hallway, it was a long hallway and I had already phoned The AP and asked for the, to me, the smartest young reporter we had there, and all the young reporters were much more lenient toward integration and all that, they were bright and right out of college, so they were ready to—and he—I said that, not that this was integration, but he was so quick and so good and I asked for him and I got whatever I wanted on that score. And he stayed on the phone during the verdict reading...

KOMOR: He kept it open.

JOHNSON: So I picked it up and I—that's how we had a 30-second beat.

KOMOR: Because he held the phone.

JOHNSON: He had the phone open.

KOMOR: Right.

JOHNSON: And I gave the verdict. And then I had—went to another phone, though, because Art Everett had to phone a lot more in and he took the phone, and so I went to another phone, there was a whole bank of them outside, and I started dictating, and then—I'm not going to mention his name because I don't believe in doing that, but this guy was a Pulitzer Prize winner and he screamed at me for my—he—they had heard, of course, I was giving—that, you know, this exclusive, and he could hear it and he said, "I want it now! I need it for A—" I said, "You—read it on the AP wires." And so he cursed me for, I mean, really stood there and cursed. I had to wait—so then I was whispering the thing, but it went out and New York was very pleased with that. And, in fact—what's the New York Times man? He's a well-known—won—four-time Pulitzer Prize winner, he said that they asked him for the story and he said, "I don't have it, she got it exclusively," you know, and I thought this was very—New York was very pleased with that. I had no idea that it would make a splash, but it was interesting. Then I had...

[*Break in recording*]

JOHNSON: Harry said I should give the other one too, because he told New York about it and somebody called us, I said, "I can't do it. I gave him my word that I would only use the one." And Harry said, "What do you care, he's a murderer." And I said, "But that's not what counts. What counts is my word," you know, "not that he's a murderer." I felt that way and I still feel that way and I have his interview in my bank vault. I may put it in my book, I don't know. But another night that is very fascinating that has never come out before and was when—we were talking with him—he would, he would—he drank, but not too heavily and I didn't take a drink at all because I had too many stories to write, although I would have liked to have one to relax but he got a little tight one night, and he said, he said, that, "[Captain Ernest L.] Medina did not give the order," this has never been in print before and I haven't—"did not, did not give the order to shoot to kill and all, all the people of—" he was charged with 22 people, but the Army said there were over 300 dead bodies and then the pictures that came out from Life magazine, if you remember, were just hundreds of bodies in the, in the ditch and so forth. And he said, "But you knew that's what he meant." And when we left his house that night, that was after one night, I was with Joe Holloway and I sai—Joe and I said, "I don't believe what I just heard." He said, "We're not going to say a word about it." Joey had been to Vietnam, and he was very sympathetic to the Army, yeah, to Calley and so forth, and he felt we should say nothing, and I said, "I've got to. I think we need to tell Boccardi." So I went, and I did call Boccardi and said, "Look, this is what he said." And of course the whole trial was predicated on the basis that Calley was acting on orders and, and he killed all these people because he'd been ordered to and here he, he told us—so Boccardi said, "Was he drunk?" And I said, "No," and he said, "Have you ever seen him drunk?" "Yes, I had one night—a couple of times." And he said, well,

"We're going to have to have more than that, because he can deny he said it and so forth, and it'll, it'll really disrupt the trial terribly. But we need to make sure. I want you to go through everything in the trial, and find what you can that, that will refute—somebody else that can confirm this sort of thing." Anyway, I spent practically all night going through a zillion notes, and I really could not find what—Boccardi was correct in doing that because we would've, you know, we didn't—we would not get into the kind of trouble that CNN got into when I was there, you remember? I don't know the story. And he had told me it was best that we should not use it, and, so, that was the end of that, we let it go. But, Calley did say that and I think it probably was the truth. He had been drinking a little bit but he wasn't drunk, you know.

KOMOR: So it probably was the truth that he had never advertently—

JOHNSON: He never really said it, but he said, "You knew that's what he meant." Well, they asked—I covered the Medina trial too, and they asked him pretty strongly, and he said, "I never gave the order. I was shocked when I saw," you know, "that." But it was, it was fascinating, it really was fascinating.

KOMOR: But Medina was not convicted, was he?

JOHNSON: No. He was freed too. He had a—a famous lawyer, I don't remember his name now.* He arrived

* Francis Lee Bailey Jr., (1933–)

from New York, at Fort Benning in this hot, hot spring, with a long-length fur coat. But anyway, and I don't think he was guilty, I don't think he gave the order, he claimed he didn't, but for Calley to say that was a, was a pretty shocking thing. So that never made print.

KOMOR: Was that '69?

JOHNSON: That was...

KOMOR: That trial?

JOHNSON: No, that was '71.

KOMOR: '71.

JOHNSON: The massacre took place in '69.* And when, when Calley was met by an officer at the plane, he thought they were going to give him a medal for what he had done. He really—I think that the Army was as much responsible for having a man like that doing it. But, when he first met the helicopters coming back, the American Division, which was—traces back to World War II, but his group was the first-hit division, his platoon was the first one there, and when they came back, they found so many boots with just legs in it, and they'd been decimated, and so it shocked him and so when they landed at My Lai, on the hill, they were ready to kill, but there were no, no there [weren't] Viet Cong there; it was just old men, women and children, and they just went crazy, you know, and were shooting wildly; not all of them, but some of them. And one

* The My Lai Massacre occurred March 16th, 1968.

of them, one of the soldiers shot himself in the foot,* rather than going—he didn't want to kill, you know, civilians, and there were just no troops there, but Calley ordered the kill and, and I think that war hardens you, makes you feel—I think he deserved to be convicted, but not to serve too long and, of course, there was a tremendous outpouring. And, and, they got a hundred thousand telegrams at the White House after he was convicted. And, I read some of the telegrams that came to Fort Benning, and it said, "He's being crucified, and I'm turning in all my medals from World War II." And, it was just a furor, and [President Richard M.] Nixon recognized that and that's why he put him under house arrest, and nobody could talk to him. For three years, he was under house arrest.

KOMOR: Did you cover him at all during that time?

JOHNSON: He was never allowed to interview.

KOMOR: I see.

JOHNSON: But when he got out, he lived in Columbus, which was, you know, my home, my native state—city, and he was getting married to, to the daughter of a well-known jeweler, the Vicks. [...] I went for that and I covered it for The AP. The thing that was sort of weird to me, a little bit, was there was about—a child about 4 years old, who was walking down the aisles with the wedding, in the wedding and, you know, Calley was—that was one of the things that came up at

* Herbert Carter (?)

the trial, that he had picked up a 4-year-old boy by the arm, and threw him in a ditch and shot.

KOMOR: And that stood in your mind. That was...

JOHNSON: That came to my mind, you know, it's kind of a—because having covered the trial I had a different reaction to it. He wasn't a profound guy, he was a decent guy. I don't think he would ever have killed in civilian life. He wasn't a murderous type, but I think the war did that to him. And he was quizzed about the, the Geneva Conventions; he had never heard of it. If he had, it made no impression on him, you know. I think that's what the Army was doing, grabbing them and throwing them over there to some extent, you know. But most people, like, like the guy in the helicopter, who saw several hundred Vietnamese hiding in, like, little caves on the side and mostly women and children and he landed, and Calley and them were coming up and he said, you know, he turned his gun on Calley and said, "You," you know, "you can't shoot." He took them out, gradually, and called in more helicopters, and some of them were injured and so forth. And this was an American helicopter—so you do get troops who, you know, had a very different reaction. But he went in thinking that, that these people were all—they were told, it was the wrong intelligence, they were told the Viet Cong were there. So it's kind of a, you know, it's, tough thing.

[*interruption*]

KOMOR: Oh, you know what? One thing that I find fascinating, just to chitchat for a moment, did you ever talk to Linda Deutsch about Art Everett and Harry Montgomery [sic.]?* Because they showed up at the Manson trial and beat a quick retreat. The same thing, and Linda was left holding the bag, and, of course, that made her career. It set her career going with Manson; that was it. She knew that she was—that was the, that was the turning point. Did you ever chat with her? Oh, Art Everett with the hankie out of—you know, and the debonair...

JOHNSON: No. Art was a great trial lawyer and well known.

KOMOR: This is why they were sent, and they were senior people, of course, but they made a quick retreat in both cases and left the women to cover the trial.

JOHNSON: Well, that happened with me too, you know, with Calley.

KOMOR: Well, that—I know, it could have—that's what—I'm sitting here, listening to this story thinking, "Now where have I heard that before?"

MURPHY: I know, "I'll come back for the verdict, you just take care of it."

JOHNSON: Yeah, well, I never thought about it.

KOMOR: Yeah, it's—but, but literally. Art, Art Everett said to Linda, "This is too much, this is insane. I can't be here. I've got to take a vacation, 'bye."

* Misspoke, should have said, "Harry Rosenthal."

JOHNSON: Well that's, that's what he did to me, yeah.

KOMOR: And they were New York types, but Harry was from Washington, I think. Was that right?

JOHNSON: Yes. Yes, yes.

KOMOR: Yeah, so one came from New York, one from Washington, and they both couldn't handle it. I mean, it, it—and Linda, you know, I interviewed Linda in, in L.A. just last week. She had the same story. Isn't that a riot, Kathryn?

JOHNSON: I didn't realize that happened to her too. It definitely happened to me, and particularly when the president decided to put, you know, Calley under house arrest, they were both gone. Well, no, first, Art was about to go, Harry had already gone.

[...] What happened is Art was—said, "Hurry, get in," and his car and through that open, the door, and we shot to where we were supposed to hear the verdict. We were going through Fort Benning, and he was up on lawns, up on the sidewalks driving crazy, and I wasn't surprised to see these blue lights flashing and the, the MPs stopped us and, so, I told him, I said, "The word is that he's being—Calley is being freed, and we're reporters." And Art starts, boy, really getting angry, you know, and the man said, "If you get nasty, I'm not going to let you all go on," and I said, I said, "Art, shut up and come on, let's go." And we went and after that when—New York was calling for all kind of stories, and Art was packed, in fact, he had his suitcases in the car, and he said, "I'm leaving." And I said, "Oh? I've got a phone call," we were at the motel while he was getting—and he said, "Tell them I've gone and don't tell them I'm here, I'm leaving." And he left, he took his bags, and I had to cover the rest by myself. We were the last reporters in Fort Benning, I'm convinced. Well, one reporter and my photographer and I, you know.

KOMOR: Tell us a little bit about that period of your work for AP, after Calley.

JOHNSON: Well then I got the POWs pretty close on that.

KOMOR: How'd that happen?

[*Tape three*]

JOHNSON: OK. Well, the first story we did on the POWs was in 1969, and, of course, the Vietnam War was raging then, and New York sent me down a three-paragraph story on the POW wives in Tidewater, Virginia, there and that's what they dealt with. And they said they wanted me to go up there and see what I could get on them.

KOMOR: Do you remember who asked you?

JOHNSON: It wasn't Boccardi. It might have been Blackman, but I'm not sure he was there then. There was another guy, well known, I'm sorry, it'll probably come to me later, but I can't think of it.

KOMOR: That's OK.

JOHNSON: And I read the three lines—I didn't even know there had been POW wives in that kind of condition, not knowing whether they were wives or widows, you know, and in fact, there had been very little even said about them anywhere in the country, because—and Charlie is—[Charlie] Kelly's widely read, and he was my photographer up there, and he didn't know much about them either. So we flew up to Virginia Beach, and I had called the head of—the woman who was head of the League of Women's—Wives of POWs or something, they had founded in Virginia.* And she arranged for, I think it was, 11 interviews in one day; I went two days at the most. And—to be held at her house and that first story, listening to those women who did not know if they were wives or widows or whether their husbands were dead, and they were living lives of not knowing about their husbands, raising children alone, and it was a really horrifying sort of story. And these women, talking to them, one at a time, all day long with—at her house and by, the way, it was—her home was near where the base is, air base, and you could hear the planes flying over, Air Force planes, all the time and it was almost the touch of the Vietnam

* Johnson visited the home of Jane Denton, who founded a local support group, like many other wives across the country. The League of Wives of American POWs, organized by Sybil Stockdale in San Diego, C.A., in 1967. Later, with the help of wives across the country, she organized the National League of Families of American Prisoners in Southeast Asia in 1970.

War still around, you know, feeling. And we were in her living room and they came in one at a time, and it was such a stream of consciousness of anguish that at the end of that day, Charlie and I both found out, we were both just shaking and we were both tough cookies, you know, but it was just—the first bride, the first wife we spoke to was a bride of two days before he was sent to Vietnam.* And the second one was a mother of six children and, another one was a mother of seven children.† And the one of six children knew that her husband was alive, but the one of seven hadn't heard. And one was—I've forgotten the—anyway, all of them were just so—oh, the only word she ever had, the possibility that her husband was alive, because they found a bloody helmet at the wreckage of his plane in North Vietnam.‡ And those were the first four we interviewed; it was really something. And by the end of the day, it was just such, so much anguish, that I asked if we could postpone the next few coming up to the next day. And these women told me, if I didn't see them that day, they couldn't gear themselves up enough to come and talk, you know. And at first, they were wary of the press, and conservative, and not wanting to talk about their situation but as time went on, and they got into it, you know,

* June Nelson, wife of Navy Lieutenant Richard Nelson.

† Louise Mulligan, wife of Captain James A. Mulligan Jr.; Jane Denton, wife of Rear Admiral Jeremiah Andrew Denton.

‡ Jean Ellison, wife of Lieutenant Commander John C. Ellison.

it was a fascinating story, but a heartbreaking story in a lot of ways. And it was the first major story anybody had, I think, because it was—AP sent it out on the A Wire as a feature, and I was told later that it was the most heavily played enterprise story of that unbelievable news year, you know, 1969, so—and from then on, that sent Charlie and me back to Virginia Beach and Tidewater, you know, Portsmouth and so forth, where the wives were, for the next four years.

We must have written, I mean, hundreds of stories and pictures. And when we got back to Atlanta, we would—he would do photos of the pictures we were taking, and I would dig through a lot of the papers and get the copies with their pictures and mail it to them, so I could stay in touch with them, you know. And we were sent up there so often that it was—I just left a packed bag, actually, as I did during the civil rights movement, in my office, so I could, you know, zip out in a hurry. What we did was, after a while we got to know the wives well, and what the children were, and who they were, and that gave us great access. Every time we went, we were able to get these women. I don't know how to begin to tell you—some of them, one of them told us how she almost committed suicide; she had a 4-year-old child, a boy, and in the—she had gone home, and it was just so awful—nobody—they treated her with such pity that she didn't like it, decided to go back to Virginia Beach—Norfolk, actually, I think, at that time, it was—so that she could have the comfort of the other wives—there were about 22 of them in that area.* And, I interviewed Jeremiah Denton's wife, Jane Denton, who was at that time a lovely, almost cameo-like beauty, blue eyes and very long hair and dark hair. She was—she had—at that time, she had seven children, and she had heard that Jerry was alive, but no other word from him. She had—her oldest son grew up enough to go to Vietnam and become a helicopter pilot himself and come back. And, one of the wives—the children were probably the most distressing. [Captain] James [A.] Mulligan, who was, who was there almost eight years, had left six young boys at home, and he was gone eight years and Louise [Mulligan] said that, "It ought to be a law against rearing boys alone." And she said that one of the boys wanted to go to a naval academy which his father had gone to, and then go back and bomb the hell out of North Vietnam, while the other one would have nothing to do with the military, was just contemptuous of Nixon and, you know, it was one administration after the other. In fact, one wife told me that her—one woman told me her son was shot down during one administration, and had gone through two more, and she hoped that he would be freed in the Nixon administration. It was just—these were heartbreaking stories to hear, you know. And

* Jane Marik, wife of Lieutenant Charles W. Marik, presumed to have died upon crashing into the South China Sea.

their children were growing up without fathers, and that was extremely touching. Charlotte Christian had three daughters, and the youngest was a year and a half when he left, and they had a big sign out front which said, "Mike Christian has been gone 4,103 days," or something like that. And they updated it every day. And then the youngest child told her, "I can't wait for Daddy to come home so I can meet my daddy." And that was kind of heartbreaking; she had no remembrance of him. And, I wrote a story about—well, this was later, but—when Christian, when they—[Stewart] had talked about it coming out, but talking about the children, one of the children was a little 3-year-old boy, and he—I was inside interviewing with his wife, the POW's wife, she didn't know whether he was dead, and it turns out he was, actually, in the long run, but we could look out the window, and there was this little 3-year-old, and a father—some father had come home in the neighborhood, and he had picked up his kids and tossed them in the air, you know, and the little—her little one was standing there like this, and the man just didn't see him, I think he would have picked him if he had noticed, but he was just totally unseeing. And then when he came home, he said, "What's a daddy?"

KOMOR: Goodness.

JOHNSON: Yeah. It was just all very touching; I wrote that up. And then another 4-year-old, he was—he didn't know his father either, but he said, "Where's my daddy?" Because he'd been hearing about it, and she said, "He's at sea," he'd been gone, missing, I think three years, and he said, "No, he's not, he's dead," you know, a little 4-year-old. They were—the women were—they didn't know whether they were wives or widowed, and there was a great deal of concern about that. And some—a few of them had met men and wanted to remarry but didn't know what—whether they had a husband or not. And then when they let out this guy [Navy Lt. Robert Franchot] Frishmann, they let out one or two POWs at one point, and when he came back to the States, he talked and told about how they were hung from the ceiling, tortured, held in stirrups, and all kind of awful stuff. And solitary confinement—Jerry Denton, who later became Senator, you know, Jeremiah Denton from Alabama, he was, he was held in solitary confinement for 42 months, and he said—and savagely beaten for about eight days for information, because he was highest ranking at that time; he was a captain.* And he refused, of course, he didn't want to talk. And he said that he was like a crippled roach, because he'd been beaten so bad. And he crawled on the floor to get his food. I mean, just unbelievable horrors, really. I learned all these things when they, when they came back. And the Mulligans—when we heard they were coming back, AP, The AP committed me to a story from—to get exclusive on Jeremiah Denton, when I

* Denton was a commander at the time of his capture.

had not even talked with him and I had had no concept of what was involved but it was just ordered; Lou Boccardi just plain ordered me to get this, eight, eight days in a row. And he said, "Well, you can give him, you can give him the right to read your—have his byline, and so you'll have to read it by him, and he'll have to approve it." Well, they thought it was, I guess, they thought it was a snap, but it was extremely difficult. They had no idea, AP nor I, of the circumstances involved with their torture and their imprisonment, and, so when...

KOMOR: Or whether they would speak at all.

JOHNSON: I know it. Well, I had no idea. So, I did ask Jerry; I went through Jane—when the men came home—they brought a few at a time, over, in '73. [...] But the—my word, they could not talk to anybody; they refused to, because they were afraid they would hurt the men that were still imprisoned. And, they—oh, and what really was fascinating to me was when they got back, when they finally were allowed to talk, I was up at—well, I had gotten at Denton but first, let me tell you, when I was trying to get him, I was in Portsmouth, and I went every day to the officers' club there, and I talked to the guys who were—each one, each man was a—each prisoner who came home was assigned a Navy guy to help him get acclimated into things, anything he needed and so forth, and I talked to them, and some of them told me things they had heard from the

POWs. But they didn't even have the sense, some of them—they had no business telling me some of those things. But I wasn't about to hurt any POW still over there, so I didn't print it. But if it had gone to the wrong reporter, that could have been a disaster, maybe. But anyway, he—I sent word through Jane, and I was told to come up to talk to the head—a Navy guy there, a commander, admiral, and then Jerry Denton. And he said, "You want this story from Jerry, but it has to be approved by the Navy." And I said, "Well, AP did the early story in '69, the first major story on the POWs, and we've written hundreds since, we've come back up here, and I think we deserve it." And a couple of the TV stations—I don't know which, Mary [Murphy], but they had offered big sums of money to Denton but he couldn't be bought at that point at all. And he said, "Well, my wife wants you to do it." And I said, "Well, we did a story," I said, on the first story—and he started quoting "Silent anguish is the common bond," about the 22 women in the Portsmouth—that's the way my story began.* And he'd been told about it, and he, you know, liked it. That's how I got him, by all the work I had done for the wives, I'm sure. And I had no idea they would ask me to do this.

But we went up first, to—I got a telephone call to be at the airport in 30 minutes, because we've got to

* "Wives of the War's Forgotten Men," Kathryn Johnson, Dec. 22, 1969, Stevens Point (Wis.) *Daily Journal*, Page 18 Column

go to Elon College for—one of their children, their seven children, was graduating and so, I made the airport and flew up with them and I had to start the first of the eight series, and it was, it was just hellish to try to get. But before I get into Jerry Denton, let me tell you about when they came home, when the POWs came home, I—Charlie and I were back up at, I think it was Portsmouth that we were landing on, Norfolk Air Force Base, and it was freezing cold, and the plane, the first plane was three hours late, and if you remember at all, you all may be too young to remember, but Jerry Denton was the first off the plane, and he stood at the microphone after nearly eight years' imprisonment, and said, well, you know, "We are happy to be home and to have served our country," and he ended up saying, "God bless America." Well, he became the eloquent symbol, really, of all the returning POWs, by that. So he was much in demand, and that's why Boccardi wanted me to get him. And, they wanted—so when I first started, we were to go to Elon for the first story, and wanted 2,000 words a day. And he went up there, and he watched his son graduate. And that was very touching too, because the son reached out and hugged him, you know, while he was talking, and then we went back to the motel at night, and I knew I had to get the story out. And Jerry took two hours to draw me a little frame here showing—this is the first year, all these years and he had complete knowledge of every torture and what it was for, and he put it down in little—above that year and the month. And on some of them went way high, and I asked, "Why is that?" And that was—the torture was so bad and so intense; he was showing the intensity of the torture. And then he explained everything; he would get on the floor and show how they did his legs and so forth, and that took two and a half hours, yeah, it was, trying to get a story. And I was trying to tape it, but after a while, he, he said he didn't want it taped, so I just had to rely totally on notes from then on. So about 3 in the morning, I had it ready, well, you know, that was thousands of words for hours of it, and meanwhile, I had ordered onion soup; that's all we had to eat all day and at 3 o'clock in the morning, I went back to their motel room, they were in bed, and I said, "I've got the story, if you just want to glance at it." And he sits up in bed, turns on the light, and starts going over it. And then Jane moved over, and I got in bed with the three of them; {laughs} I was dressed but it was the only way to keep up with them, you know. {Laughs} So the three of us—and he said, he had written down—he would—I would—he would stop, and I would, I would tell him about something, and how to change it, or I would change because he wanted it changed.

And then—he said, "Well, the lead," I had a lovely dramatic lead which any reporter would like, but he said he didn't want that, he said, "It's not—it's a soldier's story," you know, "if you get killed, you get killed." I mean, he was just a very straightforward, really wore a soldier's coat of honor. And then when we'd get to something else he wanted changed, instead of going—just keeping on going, he would go back to the start, and go all the way through it again, you know. I just had to deal—and I didn't realize—I had to deal with the terrible way he had suffered, and that—you know, eight years' imprisonment, and he hadn't been out a week, two weeks, I think. And that's what I—and New York had no idea of this, you know. So it was—I barely got it in in time for the paper, and I dictated it, I think, to New York and all of them; 2,000 words. And then I was dead tired, and then we had to go back. So every day was, was just hellish to try to get, to try to get the story. And, one of them, we went—he was going to their home for the first time, because they first went to the naval hospital, and, and stayed there for about a week. And at that time, the women were very wary and very leery of anybody writing too much about them. So I had to be really careful, and, you know, handle it very delicately. And he got out of the car, and he had a new Navy suit, and all his—six of his children, one was still in school—and he had six of his children trailing along, and he met the family dog and things were in bloom, because it was jonquils in spring, in Virginia, and he sort of stopped and looked around, and, I know it sounds weird, but at that moment, there was flight of wild geese in V formation that flew right over his house with him. Everybody, we all looked up, and it was almost like a salute, you know. And, I was supposed to go in and get him, and that was the first time he was home. So I looked at Charlie, and I said, "You know, we'll just get him later. I'm just not going to do it; I just can't break into that family again," because the night before, we'd gone to the little house they were in before they went to this—where he lived at that time. And he was—I forgot where the interview was going on, but his doctor was there, and some sort of a psychiatrist and so on and they were talking to him in front of me about how disastrous it was for him to have to do what he was doing with me, and to cut it off.

And he said, you know—he always honored his commitments, and he had made the commitment to me, so he was determined to do it and he was deter—also concerned about my welfare, you know, because we were—for eight days, I worked 20 hours a day and I remember when we went to Washington, he had to go up there for a Navy meeting, he was greatly honored, there were three or four POWs who were being honored, and there was a man in charge who would get in touch with me about when I could see Jerry to get the next story, and then—I had flown to Washington without a reservation, because I didn't know, you know, that I was even going. So they had trouble, they put me out of one room and put me into another, and two nights, there was no way, you know, that they could find a room for me, because it was crowded with all the Navy people. So, I was out writing, I had my typewriter on, and I was typing on a table, and I had my coat and everything, and the hotel—by then, they knew who I was and they were lovely, they said, "You can sleep on the sofa tonight," you know, and that's what I did for two nights. But anyway, we got it, and he said, "How about us doing one story, two stories—let's just skip one night." And I said, "No, that would break the story; we can never do it." I don't think New York ever had any idea of how difficult it was, you know, to get that. But, I jumped ahead to Jerry, because that was wildly fascinating, I mean, it got great play, and it was under his byline, which is one of the things...

KOMOR: That's fascinating.

JOHNSON: Yeah. And that was the reason I had to do all that, you know. And, he—but the reunions, I think, were some of the most poignant. After four years, I knew all about the whole families, you know, so when they were waiting. And when Jerry came home, he came down, and first, they had to go talk to that admiral at the microphone and then they could greet their wives and so forth, and he stood there, he came down, and all seven children just went over him like a wave. And his tear-streaked face kept emerging from the crowd, and they were hugging him, you know, it was very, very touching. And then Mulligan came down, and Mulligan had, had the six sons, and when he had left, one of them was 7, one was 9, and one was 13, 14, of course, that was eight years; they were young men and a couple of them had, in those years, the hippie thing, he had long hair, and I heard later that Jim Mulligan didn't like that a bit, but, {laughs} you know. And, anyway, then he started greeting his sons, by the oldest one first, and then the second one, and so on because he always had done that, his wife told me later. And that was an interesting thing. But to me, the most, I think, the most poignant was [Lieutenant Commander William Michael] Bill Study, and he had been kept in the Philippines, because they first, you know, come over in a big exodus from the Philippines, gotten into the Philippines, a few at a time, until they were all over, and he had been gone eight years, almost eight years, and his son was 4 or 5 months old when, when he left for Vietnam, and the little boy was there in a Boy Scout uniform, he was 8 years old, and shy, never knew his father, of course, and the men who had small children had been warned, "Don't touch them. Don't reach for them, because you'll scare them, they're too small." And so he—his wife came—when he came down, he came bouncing down the ramp, nice looking, big blond guy, and he came down, and he went to the microphone, and Jane broke loose from where she was, his wife, and ran to him, and he grabbed her and swung her around in an embrace; it was very touching.

Then he—she brought him over to meet the little boy, and he was holding a little American flag, in a little Boy Scout uniform, and he knelt, and she put a hand—the father knelt to be at the size, look face-to-face with the little one, and Jane put her hand on the boy's shoulder, and she said, "This is your daddy. This is your father," I think she said. And they—he sat there, and his tears were streaming down his face, and he reached out for the boy, he's not supposed to, but it was so touching, he couldn't help it. And I was standing next to Admiral Ralph Cousins, and I had been interviewing him a little bit, and he was commander of the fleet there at the time, the Atlantic fleet this time, and he—I rarely cry, and I said, "I never cry," and I was crying there. He said, "I cry over every one of them." That was kind of moving. And Charlotte Christian told me that when her husband came down, that he better not stop to talk to the admiral, and, "The admiral better not get in my way," when she first run to him {laughs}. So, they were—that was—they were hauntingly beautiful, and they were almost classics of men returning from long wars and seeing families, almost classic. But when they got home, when I was in Elon, I had to cover that night—when, finally, all the men were back in the States and they knew everybody was safe, had nobody still left being tortured because they were talking, and they were listening, in Vietnam, to everything that was being said here. So, I was—all over the United States, at the same time, they were having—or, you know, same evening, they were having the men meet, and being interviewed. And there were quite a few people—and so I had Tidewater group. And it was utterly fascinating, from all of them, all over the country. They had—they were—they talked about, you know, the long years of being in solitary and being tortured, and it was just unbelievable. One of them, who had his leg—no, his arm was very badly burned and he said there were so many—the flies were on it, and they were only washing it out twice a week, the Vietnamese, and it was getting worse, he was afraid he was going to lose it. So he saw flies flying around, and he let them—he held his arm out and let the flies land on it, and they laid eggs, and they came out as maggots at first, and the maggots ate all the dead skin off. And after that happened, to get rid of them, because he couldn't get water, except when the Vietnamese brought it in, he went over to the barrel, and he urinated on his arm to get rid of the maggots. And that did, it got rid of them and then he wrapped it up with his shirt. And that was the beginning of the healing for his arm. I mean, some of the stories were just unbelievable, you know, that we heard that night.

Then—let's see—after Jerry's—well, I don't know what all you wanted. There's so many stories about the POW wives that I think of. I could just go on and on with the old thing. But, you know, the torture was really unreal, and some of them would get on the floor and demonstrate what they did to them. Like this guy [Commander Richard A.] Stratton in California, he had—they tied the back of his legs to his arms in the back, and he was held so long that he couldn't make use of either one of his arms. And the roommate he had, another POW, he took care of him for a year just like a baby, he said, he couldn't—had no use of his arms. And how they could come home and have the will to survive, and to try to last, to me, it was very amazing, very touching. I think it took enormous courage, and every one of them admitted, except Jerry Denton and they really put Jerry out, 'cause they—that's why he was tortured so badly, because had such a strong spiritual sense, he really felt that he couldn't do that, you know, and that's why he was badly beaten. But practically every man there said he was broken. Well, you had to, after a while. And besides, they didn't give out any information that wasn't available in most Army magazines, or that kind of magazine, in this country, you could get it. So that was a fascinating story.

KOMOR: And that preoccupied you for several years?

JOHNSON: That preoccupied me for four years.

KOMOR: Yeah. Four years.

JOHNSON: Yeah. From '69 until they were freed. And even after that, I had to go in and talk to some of them. One of them committed suicide; he was very quiet and he talked very little, and after four months, he committed suicide. And people like [Captain William Porter]

Bill Lawrence, who came back to take command of the naval air station—the Naval Academy, I went up to talk to him, and his wife had divorced him while he was in prison. He said, "I should have expected it, but I didn't." And then there was some—several of them like that but most of them had wives waiting for them, and did really well, considering, you know. But I know, when I was talking to Jerry, they had—there were a couple of POWs there, one night, and the man's house we were having the interview with, his dog came out and walked across and both the POWs who were talking, they stopped cold and watched [the] dog walk all the way across and another time they stopped was the chiming of the clocks, I couldn't help but notice, and I found out when I talked with them later, they couldn't—for so many years in solitary, that they had hung onto it if they saw a little rat going across the floor, and some of them even saved pieces of crumbs from their bread so they could give to the rats, because they're the only creatures they saw, anything except the...

[*break in recording*]

KOMOR: Kathryn, during the mid-'70s, you, you were still in Atlanta, is that right?

JOHNSON: Yeah.

KOMOR: For AP?

JOHNSON: Yeah.

KOMOR: And let's see. You went to Harvard as a Nieman [fellow].

JOHNSON: Yeah.

KOMOR: Was that '75 or '76?

JOHNSON: '76, '77. I went in '76 and finished in '77.

KOMOR: '76, '77. And was there something that stands out for you about that year that you'd like to tell us and, and how you transitioned back to AP and then when you decided to leave? You want to talk about that?

JOHNSON: Yeah. Well, I wasn't—I didn't even apply until three weeks before the deadline because of Hal Goldman who was the editor of the Atlanta Constitution kept insisting; he thought that I should apply. And he got the people to write for me; you have to get people to write for you, about nine or 10 people. And, I was really surprised. I didn't think I would get it, but I did. I went there in the fall of '76 and a lot of them— there were some very interesting people there. They accept 12 American reporters, and they were reporters, now they're taking technicians and photographers and people that—they're spreading out which they should do, but they didn't at that time, and they took six foreigners, I say foreigners, Ted Turner at CNN told us you can never use the word "foreign." {Laughs} But—and I say that now, but when I went back—when I went there, it was a social and intellectual feast for the whole year; it really was. And a lot of them got the chance for the first time to relax and do and not study, and you only had to take one, but I audited, I took two courses and audited three because it was so fascinating; it really was. And one of the courses I took was a year of law, because I'd covered so many trials, I felt it would be good to learn more, and one of them was taught by a man from the, used to be with The New York Times, and he, Tony Lewis, and it was his course, and every time he'd get on civil rights, he'd throw his arm out and—to me and ask me a question in front of this huge crowd of students, you know. So I really had to go back to the library and bone up on what I'd been covering to make sure.

But, anyway, it was a fascinating year and at the end I was one of six who got to go to Japan and that was another thing. Having lost an uncle—well, badly, so badly, at Okinawa, he would turn up a year later in a hospital in Australia but was burnt terribly from the neck down and deaf and he was only—I thought he was old at the time—he was only 26 then, at the time he was shot down; it was on a destroyer that was torn apart—at a—by a kamikaze. And I had such a feeling against the Japanese because of, of that, and my brother was slightly injured and came back still a teenager, you know, in World War II, and so I, I didn't feel very kindly about going to Japan, and so I insisted on paying my own way and I would not accept the Japanese government paying anything. And I drove them crazy during the whole couple of months {laughs} because I would go up and insist on paying my own hotel bill, and The

AP was sending some of it, I think they sent a thousand, but it was a lot more, but it was OK, I appreciated that, but I—that was a really a tough thing to go through. But I also, I found that they were extremely honest. One of the men had brought—we were supposed to bring gifts for the Japanese, and he'd brought seven bottles of magnum scotch, the really good scotch, and he had left it in the lobby, so it disappeared for three days. And three days later I had a knock on the door, and I don't know why it was me, because I hadn't left, but they, you know, opened—I guess I had gave them so much trouble paying that they, they brought all the scotch over to me. Somebody had turned it in and given it back and they were lovely and they gave us a car each and we had interviews. We each had a Mercedes with a—take us around all day, and it was a, it was quite interesting. And at the, at the end of that, now, I went back, I went back to Harvard and then, to say, to say goodbye, but that was a wonderful year and then—we had been—we'd given their word—our word that we would spend a year wherever we left—like I'd been at AP and I never intended to leave AP, I, you know, I'd gotten wonderful assignment and although I was worked very hard and there's no question, as a woman, I really had a rough time.

[...] When I got the first Associated Press Managing Editor Award, you know, they don't give but a few of those every year, and, of course, you know, between the civil rights and Vietnam, I mean, they were just—and I got an honorable mention and I had been off for a couple of days and when I came in it was—there was a little paper, a silv—that was the reward, you know, in silver and it was in my mailbox with the end torn out, you could see it torn off, and I opened—that's when I found out that I'd won an APME Award, and of course my fellow colleagues, there were some lovely guys and they congratulated me, and I never heard a word from, from the boss. And so about two years—a year later I got another one. I think it was the Calley, I guess it was the Calley trial, and...

KOMOR: APME?

JOHNSON: And he sent me an email, through the, we had computers, then, in Atlanta, and it said that he wanted me to talk to several new—to give a little speech about winning this award because there were two new staffers he wanted them to see what they could do and that kind of thing, you know. So I messaged him back that I wouldn't talk but that, that please—and he wanted—didn't give me the award, you know, and I said, "Please leave, leave my award in the traditional way that it's left," {laughs} which was nasty of me in a way, but he really had it coming, you know, because another time when an airliner made a stop on a, on a street in—out on the outskirts of Atlanta and there were a number of injuries and I don't remember, a few dead, but it saved a lot of lives by landing that way, and so I had gotten word ahead, it was a Sunday, I was alone except for one radio guy and that's all he did every hour, he was very busy all the time, and, so I heard about the airliner and so I quickly knocked out—somebody had phoned in, and I'd forgotten who it was, and so I knocked out a couple of quick graphs, which was all that I really had, got it on the A Wire and then called in somebody for help and called in another reporter to go to the scene because we didn't know what kind of cra— how bad it was and so forth, that's big news, you know, and I called the bureau chief because I'd been told to. I did everything I was supposed to do and I went back to this young guy who was on radio, I said, "Just forget that now, and answer the phone and anything coming in on the air crash." So I went back and said, "What have you done?" And he said, "Nothing." You know, he was just frozen, he hardly spoke to me too, young guy, young kid, and he just froze. And so I pushed him aside and started handling it, you know, until we got some more people in and then the next day I got called in, the boss—for the boy and me, and he said—had him explain, and he told the boss, honestly, he said, "I froze, and I, I couldn't, I couldn't say a word." And he said, "I couldn't do it, Kathryn said—" it's very honest—and so then he turns around and he says, "Well, I blame Kathryn. I don't blame you. She should've handled it, not—" I mean, you know, I'd done everything the way I was supposed to, and I'd had an awful lot of that and so I think he had it coming about the award. {Laughs}

Although, I don't usually operate that way but, anyway. You wanted to ask about some of the AP stuff. So when I got back from—and I even got graded at Harvard, and I got an A minus, which I thought was pretty good up there, you know, because was enjoying myself too, but I audited three and took—that and political science. And immediately, we had another bureau chief then, this guy just—gotten sick of Autry and he put me on week—on night work again and weekends because he'd heard I, I didn't know him well, I could take fast dictation and so I was, I was taking dictation on the Georgia Tech football. {Laughs} Because the guys would [be] phoning in, you know, and I knew how to take football jazz, because I'd been around AP so long at it. But after a year, and, and here I was trying to make myself a better reporter for AP and I just—I stuck it with them for a year, because I promised, I gave my word to Harvard. And after that, U.S. News asked me if I wanted to be bureau chief in Atlanta. And, I wasn't too fascinated with the magazine but they offered me a big fat salary and I had a brother who was—we didn't know had had a brain tumor, and he was dying, and he had a family and I was helping them and it was just a good thing to have, you know, more money and whatnot.

And I stayed with them for a year and then when [President James (Jimmy) Earl] Carter, Carter, Carter had already—people had knew he was going to run and it had been announced, but he and Jody Powell, his new news editor, they came by the office one day, it was rainy and asked for me to go with them so he could announce for the presidency more efficiently and I said "I can't go, I'm busy and it's raining!" I never dreamed Carter would ever make {laughs}—so, but anyway, I had to go because they asked me, you know, so—and I went with them and that was a fascinating—and by that time, I just felt that it was better for me to get out of AP, and I didn't say any—anything why, although Boccardi was willing to transfer me to Washington when I first, you know, got home for the year—that was—that same fall but I had given my word, plus Mother was beginning to go downhill a little bit, but she wasn't that bad and I really wanted to go to Washington, so, but I couldn't, I just felt I couldn't go then until things got a little bit better with my brother and mother, and, and so when U.S. News came out, I felt I was able to go although they weren't exactly better, but things were in better shape, you know, and I had a nurse for Mother and my sister-in-law had moved closer and so forth to see about Mother and so forth. Anyway, I went to Washington and—that's why I left AP. I really didn't want to leave, but I didn't feel that I had any kind of future left there except to be a utilitarian, and even when they talked about sending me to Washington, they said, "You have to work a year of nights to get the hang of it." Well, I'd already been covering politics; I'd covered Carter, he was president then, I was—I covered him as state senator and as a governor, and you know—and I knew the whole crowd, the "Georgia Mafia," I guess they thought I was part of it. And I was— would've been valuable on that score, and so I just felt like I just, you know, it was just time to get out. And also the magazine was extremely rewarding financially and I could—I got off weekends and nights and holidays for the first time in umpteen years. Carter was—he's really a very good man, and really a great ex-president, you know, but he was a micromanager and, and I remember I wanted—I was a big tennis player at that time, and Jack Nelson of the L.A. Times and I were—he said, "Bring your tennis clothes and we can change at the White House and then go and play on the tennis courts." And, so I got ready and then no—nobody was playing but nobody could find out who had—who was supposed to play because Carter carried it in his pocket—who was supposed to be on the, on the team, I mean on the courts. And he, you know, he even handled the, the tennis courts.

[*interruption*]

KOMOR: Kathryn, you were talking about covering Carter on the tennis courts because—and Carter had in his pocket?

JOHNSON: Yeah, he had the, the thing that you had

to find out who was supposed to be playing tennis on—and he didn't, and he wasn't even guarding the tennis courts.

That's how much of a micromanager he was, so we were scared to go out there, you know, to go out and do it. And one of the big problems he had was he didn't trust any of the senators, the Democratic senators who were there and offered to help him. He brought his own people with him and they weren't used to Washington at all. I think my worst experience with Carter was not on a story, but it was in Plains, Georgia, when we were down there, and he was a pitcher, and he was very competi—competitive even on the baseball court, and he was pitching and Jody was catcher and I was on third base and I'm no great player, but I knew how to play baseball, I could catch pretty well. Somebody hit a ball and it came right to me. Well, the sun was in my eyes and I missed it, and it went right down. And Carter turned around and put his hands on his hips and stared at me a fully 20, 30 seconds. And I'm, like, it was embarrassing, it really was. And he had those green eyes, cold, we used to call it the "double whammy," you know, he—and after that inning ended, I asked to be taken off {laughs}; it was tough going. But, his mother, I covered her, she was a delight, too, Lillian Carter. There used to be these little things on the back of the cars. There was—one of them that said, "Miss Lillian was right,

Billy [William Alton Carter] is smarter." {Laughs} [...] I had gone to something in downtown Atlanta when she was—to make a speech, and—oh, Phil Donahue brought his crew down for his TV thing for her, and he said, "Well, I understand that you had a—that you enjoyed a drink at night but you couldn't get one in the White House." And she said, "Who says that?" He said, "Well, it's supposed to be dry. The whole White House, we were told, is dry." And she said, "Well, listen, I had a drink every night and I don't know where it came from, but I had a drink every night." And before she went out, I was in the, in the back with her and trying to find out if I could see her again by herself away from TV, and, you know, and her slip kept falling down, half of it. So finally, and I was taking it, pinning it up for her while trying to interview her and finally it came down again before she went out so she just reached down and yanked it off. And, and handed it to me and there were a lot of Georgia Tech college students in the crowd, and they came up to me after, saw that I was holding Miss Lillian's slip and was going to give it back to her, and they said, "We'll give you money for that!" {Laughs} It was so funny. But she was an offbeat—in a way, I felt sorry for Jimmy Carter 'cause they were just wildly individualistic, you know, and said almost anything, I'm sure they embarrassed him somewhat, but he never showed it and he never said anything like that.

[*Tape four*]

JOHNSON: I'll tell you one interesting thing about Carter when I was with the magazine. One problem I had with the magazine was they published once a week and I was so used to breaking news that when, for example, remember when that plane landed in the Potomac and killed all those people, I just was so anxious to go there and they didn't want nobody to go there because it happened early in the week and we had plenty of time, you know, to get all the details. But with Carter, when the hostages were being kept and they had the helicopters, you remember, and he was hoping to get them freed, and of course it didn't work out, but I got a phone call from Jody Powell and he said they were all going to meet at the White House and go for a drink and then go back and see Carter, because everybody was hopeful, you know. I wasn't assigned to do that, because I was U.S. News and there was nobody at the White House that night. We would find out what happened the next morning, you know. And I just wasn't geared to that. So I went to the White House and Carter was sitting behind the desk and with a—he had his hand on the phone like he expected a phone call, you know, for it to come through. And we went out, we crossed Lafayette Square, that's before they closed it all off to, you know, people, demonstrators and people, who were going to hurt the White House so we went across Lafayette Square and had a drink that night and got back about 3 o'clock in the morning and went in, and Carter was still there with his hand on the phone. It was kind of, {laughs} you know, and it was obvious they weren't going to call. They waited till [President Ronald] Reagan got in, then they...

KOMOR: Yeah.

JOHNSON: They got it and, you know, and I didn't cover much of Reagan. I mostly filled in when they needed me over at the White House. And there were a lot of things about the Hill that came in and I had to go. And, of course, I knew—I didn't—I could usually get an interview with Carter when some of the other people, you know, not necessarily couldn't, but it wasn't hard. I knew Jody pretty well, you know, from Atlanta. So he—what was so interesting to me is we went—let me get to Reagan.

Reagan, when I was covering the White House that day, Reagan, we were supposed to interview him, and we asked all these questions, and I had a bunch of them and we were talking to him and then Nancy Reagan comes in and she says, "It's time for your portrait to be painted." And here we had a, you know, really, meeting with, going on with news people and he looked at her, looked at us, and threw up his hands, got up and did what she said, you know. And I wondered and looking back, if his Alzheimer's wasn't beginning, you know, then, that he was you know swayed so easily sort of. I don't know. All I know is when the Democrats were in, with Carter, and they would have dinner or something, they would always—the press would be behind the ropes but they would bring us food. And every time the Republicans were in we never got a taste of food, {laughs} yeah, we would go sit up way up in the balcony at the White House. And, when Gorb—not Gorbachev, Dubinsky* [sic.] was ambassador and Reagan gave a big lovely dinner for him, you know, and they would drink and eat and all these Russians came up and had him sign their menus. And that worried me, because I thought they're going to get [an] exact copy of Reagan's signature. I didn't know—I wondered how smart that was. I don't know, you know. That was just a guess. But we were sitting up. And all that food was just looked superb. And we didn't get a bite {laughs}. Not that we expected it but you know what I mean.

KOMOR: Now when did you go to...

JOHNSON: CNN?

KOMOR: Yeah. Tell me about that.

JOHNSON: Well, the national—I knew nothing about TV writing but the national editor of CNN was a former UPI guy and he knew me and he asked me to come and interview.

KOMOR: Who was he?

JOHNSON: Paul Varian. And, so I did and he wanted me to write; just write, no reporting.

---

* Anatoly Dobrynin was the Soviet ambassador to the U.S. from 1962 to 1986. Yuri Dubinin was the ambassador from 1986 to 1990.

Of course, I don't have a TV background and believe me, that is different and you really have to have it. But I could, you know, read real fast and write fast and that's what they needed; that's what they wanted was a writer. And so I got on and that's what I did. And I was on their war team. They chose a few people to write real fast. For five weeks we couldn't—there were sandwiches as close as I am to, you know, five feet away and I was unable to find time to even go grab a sandwich, but it was interesting. I enjoyed CNN. And, it was a hard place to work in many ways because, you know, they claim much as—they were very good to me and I love CNN, I won't say that—and I still am listed as a freelancer for them but I've only worked a few weeks a year now, but I used to work an awful lot after I quit them too, but they call themselves the most trusted name in news, but they really aren't. It really is The AP is the—I think, having been in different you know as far as...

KOMOR: Why? Why is that, Kathryn?

JOHNSON: Because I think, I think AP checks and rechecks news and checks the facts and tries to go from every angle and when they don't they get caught badly and they jump on whoever did it. And early on I learned that, and I think that—I've never seen any outfit that, particularly, from the best reporters, anyway, they're really good reporters worked so hard to find the best obtainable truth and then they go with that instead of just going out, you know, like Tom Johnson did on the Olympic bombing. I don't think I...

KOMOR: Talk about that a little bit.

JOHNSON: Well, Tom, I don't want to talk about Tom, but he, he was a—former L.A. Times, I think, and he had a news background, but he was head of CNN then and he—I was standing there right next to him and he handed a newspaper, Atlanta Journal Magazine, which named the suspect for the bombing during the Olympics, you know, in '96, and he handed it to the—those two poor anchors up there and they looked befuddled, you know, because he wanted them to read from that about who was suspected, not necessarily credit the papers, I don't guess, but whatever, and so I turned to him, I said, "Have we checked this out? That's just out in the papers. It was an extra." And he said, "Oh, no, these are fine writers." Well, CNN got in all kind of Dutch from that; had to pay out millions. And this guy sued them; it took years to do but he sued them.* And that lessened my initial respect, you know. But I also found many men there and women who were real fine journalists and tried very hard. And the women were treated very poorly early on when I was working with them. And, they didn't make enough money—I guess it wasn't enough money, at the time, to live on their

---

* Richard Jewell, security guard who was wrongly accused of the July 27th, 1996, bombing in Centennial Olympic Park at the summer Olympics in Atlanta, Georgia.

own. A couple of them—some of them, six together in a little apartment, you know. It's very different now but I don't guess they had the money early on. And by that time I didn't need it, you know what I mean, I wasn't a young reporter, I was just...

KOMOR: You weren't starting out.

JOHNSON: Yeah. So, but I enjoyed it. They got in a lot of hot water too on a couple of things. Which if they had exercised some good news judgment they never would have gotten into, you know, so...

KOMOR: But do you, do you still feel that you're an AP-style journalist?

JOHNSON: Yeah, I think so, yeah. I think so. The magazine was the most generous to me and wonderful and I really loved it and all but I was geared to much more active news. And, I was so fortunate in getting some wonderful assignments from AP, despite all the nine years, I think, of working Christmas, with having one Christmas off. And my sister was there with her children and I wanted to see the little ones on Christmas morning, and I never got to, you know, and that kind of thing. But it wasn't—it was—when I got into being sent out it was all—that was very fascinating and that was worth it. So I think, basically, yes. And for a long time AP was—I would be calling them when I'd see a mistake, you know, or something {laughs} and they would take it. Now, I don't know anybody much to call. AP had dealt very—at that time the general desk dealt very harshly with people who made major errors and that's how they learned, I think. My—I suppose those three things, the Calley trial and civil rights, of course, and the POWs for four years, those were probably the most interesting. But I got many interesting assignments, otherwise, it was just, you know, around Georgia and so forth.

KOMOR: Are you still doing some writing now? You doing some writing?

JOHNSON: Do I what?

KOMOR: Do you still do some writing now? Some news writing or are you...?

JOHNSON: I'm still listed as a freelancer at CNN, but they've gotten very tight on money {laughs} and they have to. It was—I really would not want to say much, but AOL–Time Warner was a mistake and AOL was a bigger mistake and the brass at CNN knew it but there's nothing they could do it about it. That's mostly what's happening that's wrong with news business today, I think, is corporate people get into the news business and what they want is to make money and it didn't really matter that much in the past. The AP, I think it felt they could pay everybody off and do OK, that was what they wanted. At least I never felt any kind of corporate pressure, ever. It was just on the news judgment, you know.

KOMOR: Anything you want to ask?

MURPHY: Yeah, I just wanted to—you said you

wanted to go—you wanted to write, that was your initial impulse in high school?

JOHNSON: Yeah, oh yeah, I always wanted to write.

MURPHY: But I'm curious to know, I mean, you talk like you're a great writer, I can tell that, but what do you think makes a great reporter? Can you just talk a little bit about that? Because I think one is learned perhaps and one is not, you know?

JOHNSON: Yeah. Well I'm not a great writer. I'm a good writer and I've refined it.

MURPHY: Well, I can tell you're a vivid writer.

JOHNSON: Well, I, you know, you have to—in AP they went over your copy very carefully and so forth and you really, you know, you learn or you study others. But I read some great writers and I can't match those. But, I think being curious is one of the biggest things and being interested in people and even concerned, you know, about events, and being out of yourself. There's so many reporters that their intent is primarily to get before a camera, you know. I've had people ask me why, that when King was shot to death and I was in Coretta's house, the SCLC sent in a cameraman, just one camera guy, it was a young guy, and we only went for SCLC, nobody ever had a picture in the bedroom, but when I saw him with the camera I rolled out of the way because I thought it was tasteless for me to—inappropriate for me to be on the floor, you know, people wonder what is a white woman doing there. And you have to be selfless in that sense and not be trying to advance yourself, which I do think—I see that in a lot of young reporters today, you know. There's so many things that are wrong in journalism today, I think. But I don't...

MURPHY: I'm shocked by your humanity, that your humanity was in evidence on every story you do and did. And there's more of a ruthless kind of culture now in a way.

JOHNSON: Yes, that's very true. I was just very happy doing it, that's all I know. And I got totally absorbed in it and as I told you when I—after the Calley trial I couldn't believe four and a half months had gone by, it was spring, and what had happened? I didn't even remember Christmas, but I had gone home for Christmas. I think you have to have, you know, some sort of basic horse sense too, about things. I once had a young girl from AP who was going to cover some demonstrators with me and there were a lot of peace groups and when she met me back at the office and she was wearing this great big thing that's calling her a peace activist, you can't do that and be a reporter and I yanked it off and told her she couldn't go cover anything with me anymore, you know, so.

KOMOR: Kathryn, anything else you want to add?

JOHNSON: Not at the moment. I was trying to think of some things that are interesting. But I'm not sure that, you know—I'm not sure I should say them.

KOMOR: Well, thank you, Kathryn.

JOHNSON: You're welcome. Well, I've enjoyed it, I enjoyed it very much. Well, thank you. Enjoyed it.

KOMOR: This has been a wonderful experience for us. Thank you. Thank you so much.

Compiled by Sarit Hand, Coordinator, The Associated Press Oral History Program, AP Corporate Archives. 2007 Jul 18.

APPENDIX B

ORIGINAL WIRE TRANSMISSIONS

from the AP Corporate Archives

NIGHT LEAD
KING
BY KATHRYN JOHNSON

ATLANTA, MAY 15 (AP)- DR. MARTIN LUTHER KING JR. HAS PROPOSED A VAST ATTACK ON POVERTY, A "BILL OF RIGHTS FOR THE DISADVANTAGED," WHICH HE SAYS WOULD IMMEDIATELY TRANSFORM THE CONDITIONS OF NEGRO LIFE--AS WELL AS MILLIONS OF WHITE POOR.

THE NEGRO LEADER SAID HE PLANS TO TAKE HIS PROPOSAL, WHICH CALLS FOR A BROADER ATTACK ON POVERTY THAN PRESIDENT JOHNSON HAS PROPOSED, TO THE PRESIDENT IN A MONTH OR SO.

NIGHT LEAD: KING

May 15, 1964

Atlanta, May 15 (AP) – Dr. Martin Luther King Jr. has proposed a vast attack on poverty, a "Bill of Rights for the disadvantaged," which he says would immediately transform the conditions of Negro life—as well as millions of white poor.

The Negro leader said he plans to take his proposal, which calls for a broader attack on poverty than President Johnson has proposed, to the President in a month or so.

King, president of the Southern Christian Leadership Conference, told the Associated Press in an interview:

"Economists concerned with poverty feel we could do it with about $15 billion. The President's bill is only a beginning."

The administration's poverty bill calls for $962.5 million.

"So many people see life as a long corridor with no hope. This bill would give them a new sense of hope, self-respect and dignity."

The Negro leader said his proposal is patterned after the GI Bill of Rights which compensates veterans for certain advantages of which they were deprived.

"Certainly the Negro has been deprived of so much because of his legacy of slavery and deprivation.

"I don't see any possibility of bringing the Negro into the mainstream of American life without some type of compensatory consideration," King added.

"We need the kind of massive assistance program that would bring aid to between 30 and 40 million poverty-stricken people in this country. Percentage-wise, Negroes are [a]mong the largest numbers."

King said a large stratum of "forgotten white poor" would also be rescued by his bill.

Through it, he said, the government would provide educational opportunities and grants of assistance, extend the manpower training act, provide better housing conditions as well as reduce down payments for houses, and provide medical care.

King said there is a hard core of Negro poverty in the North, where Negroes have migrated by the thousands.

He added that the civil rights bill now before the Senate deals mainly with problems in the South. "It doesn't touch problems in the North."

king 2-2-2

church where only five days ago many of the nation's leading figures, including all major presidential candidates, gathered to pay a final tribute to the slain civil rights leader.

About 20 white persons were s.attered among the crowd.

Occasionally, rain splashed through open windows.

The elder King, who for many years had co-pastored the Ebenezer Church with his famous son, began his sermon by ~~stating:~~ saying "I'm not going to let the devil put me in a corner. My head is blooded but unbowed."

MRS. KING

April 9, 1968

Atlanta, Ga. (AP) – The widow of Dr. Martin Luther King Jr. told an Easter congregation at Ebenezer Baptist Church Sunday that continuing her husband's unfinished work would be the greatest tribute to him.

Mrs. King, wearing a black dress and hat, took the pulpit briefly after Dr. Martin Luther King Sr. had finished a joyful sermon on "The Resurrection."

"I know that all of you today feel with me the full meaning of Easter," Mrs. King told the more than 1,000 persons jammed into the humble red brick church where funeral services for her husband were held.

"You came here to find comfort in the crucifixion, in the resurrection and in redemption," she said. "And this redemptive feeling will continue in the world—and this is the thing most needed in the world today.

"In my heart," she continued, "I feel it is God's will for his work to go on. Our dedications and concern to the task of finishing his unfinished work will be the greatest tribute to my husband, Dr. Martin Luther King Jr."

Despite a light rain, chairs had to be set up in the aisles to accommodate the large crowd at the modest church where only five days ago, many of the nation's leading figures, including all major presidential candidates, gathered to pay a final tribute to the slain civil rights leader.

About 20 white persons were scattered among the crowd.

Occasionally, rain splashed through open windows.

The elder King, who for many years had co-pastored the Ebenezer Church with his famous son, began his sermon by saying, "I'm not going to let the devil put me in a corner. My head is blooded but unbowed."

The gray-haired pastor spoke of the thousands of letters the church has received since his son's death, and told how they expressed sorrow, interest in the church and praise for the choir, which was heard internationally on television during funeral services for King.

The elder King told the congregation that it had not yet been decided where the body of his son "would be settled." He told of an offer from Morehouse College, where his son graduated, for a tomb in a special memorial chapel. Then he added: "We have not yet made a decision. But he definitely will be moved from the cemetery."

King told the congregation, "These are mysterious and perilous times in which we live. And, many times, our hopes are shattered.

"But never lose your faith—keep your faith," he said. "You may have come here frustrated this morning, but He (the Lord) stands ready to help. He's such a good and kind Savior. I love Him.... I love the Lord.... I do."

King spoke of Jesus raising Lazarus from the dead and of how the Lord had to focus the eyes of Martha, Lazarus' sister, on the resurrection.

"Faithless people are as old as the family of man," King said. "This is not a day of death. This is a day of triumph. This is Easter morning, and one of these days all of God's children are going to get up."

"Yes, yes," a refrain rose from the audience.

"We're not serving a dead God," he continued. "I'm not serving a dead God. You tell me about a dead God after all I've gone through this past week. He's got me standing up here.

"Then don't tell me God is asleep," he said. "This is Easter morning. Oh, yes, He's up. He's up."

"He's up, He's up," several voices sang.

"He loves all of us," King said. "I love the Lord. As long as I live, I'll love the Lord."

Abruptly, he shut his Bible and walked over to the side of the church where his wife, the widow of his son and other relatives sat.

The choir burst into the song, "Oh, How I Love Jesus," and as they sang, King would occasionally chime in with an extemporaneous phrase.

"He tells me of His precious blood..." sang the choir.

"Oh, yes, He does," King said.

"There's a name I love to hear..." the choir sang.

"It sounds like music in my ear," King said.

He ended with a simple, "God bless you."

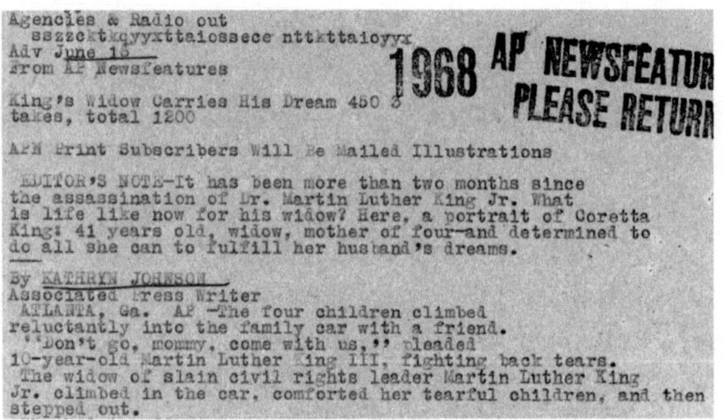

Agencies & Radio out
sszzcktkqyyxttaiossece nttkttaioyyx
Adv June 16
From AP Newsfeatures

1968 AP NEWSFEATUR
PLEASE RETURN

King's Widow Carries His Dream 450 3
takes, total 1200

APN Print Subscribers Will Be Mailed Illustrations

EDITOR'S NOTE-It has been more than two months since the assassination of Dr. Martin Luther King Jr. What is life like now for his widow? Here, a portrait of Coretta King: 41 years old, widow, mother of four-and determined to do all she can to fulfill her husband's dreams.

By KATHRYN JOHNSON
Associated Press Writer

ATLANTA, Ga. AP -The four children climbed reluctantly into the family car with a friend.

''Don't go, mommy, come with us,'' pleaded 10-year-old Martin Luther King III, fighting back tears.

The widow of slain civil rights leader Martin Luther King Jr. climbed in the car, comforted her tearful children, and then stepped out.

KING'S WIDOW CARRIES HIS DREAM

June 16, 1968

EDITOR'S NOTE – It has been more than two months since the assassination of Dr. Martin Luther King Jr. What is life like now for his widow? Here, a portrait of Coretta King: 41 years old, widow, mother of four—and determined to do all she can to fulfill her husband's dreams.

ATLANTA, Ga. AP – The four children climbed reluctantly into the family car with a friend.

"Don't go, mommy, come with us," pleaded 10-year-old Martin Luther King III, fighting back tears.

The widow of slain civil rights leader Martin Luther King Jr. climbed in the car, comforted her tearful children, and then stepped out.

She had to address a rally of the Poor People's Campaign. And neither tears, fear nor family have kept Coretta King from aiding the cause started by her husband.

That resolute will has carried her through the kaleidoscopic events and emotions since King's assassination April 4.

The man accused of the murder, James Earl Ray, was arrested in London June 6 and the U.S. government quickly started extradition proceedings to return him to Tennessee for trial.

The attractive 41-year-old window says: "I feel I have a definite role to play in carrying on. When he was alive, I played mostly a supporting role." Now she feels it has changed to one far more active.

"I'm more convinced than ever of the rightness of our cause. I'm more determined now than ever that my husband's dream will become a reality."

Many expect Mrs. King to take an even more active role in the Southern Christian Leadership Conference, which her husband founded.

Her unfaltering composure and controlled grief during the days following her husband's murder stirred the hearts of millions.

"I think you rise to the occasion in a crisis, I think the Lord give you strength when you need it," she told a friend shortly after King's death. "God was using us—and now he's using me, too."

Even as a grieving widow, she interrupted her mourning to lead a march in Memphis, where her husband had been shot to death. That day, she mingled with striking garbage collectors and the next with dignitaries and celebrities from over the land, who came to her husband's funeral in Atlanta.

Mrs. King leaned back in a large chair in her bedroom, tilted her head to one side and said with a gentle smile: "Everyone who knows me knows I'm strong-minded."

Clad in a long pink and flowered robe, her dark hair falling to her shoulders, Mrs. King was replying to friends who were urging her not to go to Memphis for the march.

"I'll continue to do those things which I feel are necessary for the continuance of my husband's work—and this means many things," she added.

It has meant:

—Flying to Memphis, with three of her children, to lead the silent march of thousands in honor of her slain husband and to plead for his cause.

—Flying to California a few days ago to enlist Hollywood support of the Poor People's Campaign—which her husband planned.

—And, on Mother's Day, linking arms with marchers in Washington and walking in the rain through the city's worst slums and past riot-damaged buildings to kick off the Poor People's Campaign.

SCLC leaders, fearful for her safety, had asked her

not to go to Memphis for the march, but she told them when she got there: "I come to you today because I was compelled. During my husband's lifetime I have always been at his side when he needed me. And today I feel he would have wanted me to be here."

Sitting in her large airy bedroom near the little booklined alcove where her husband wrote many of his speeches. Mrs. King spoke of the book she is writing of her life with her husband.

Because of her contract, she is granting no interviews until it is published, possibly by the end of the year.

She hired a secretary only after the death of her husband—and she could use three. So heavy are the demands on her time and energy that she has had to greatly enlarge her house staff. Some are volunteer SCLC workers who daily sort, catalogue and file the overwhelming mail that still pours into the house.

Occasionally, when a message is particularly poignant—and this is frequent—it is brought to Mrs. King. She hopes to read them all some day—and to answer every one.

"Do you think there'll ever be enough time in my life to do it?" she asked.

Mrs. King says she has been deeply touched by some of the gifts which have come to her. Many are paintings and sculptured busts of her husband.

Since the assassination, her nine-room redbrick

home, in a lower income neighborhood, has been full of people—and jammed with phone calls.

She has had to put in a telephone system like a switchboard which takes up to six calls at one time. And an intercom has been put on the front door so that callers may identify themselves.

Long close to her four children, Mrs. King does not try to overprotect them. Nor does she want special treatment for them. She has insisted they take part in open marches.

When Yolanda, her 12-year-old—the eldest—was recently named to an honor council at her school, her mother took time out from her arduous schedule to attend.

Long ago, Mrs. King had prepared her children to understand about their father's going to jail—and for his death. She took them with her in August, 1962, to visit him in jail in Albany, Ga.

Racial segregation deeply troubled young Coretta Scott when, as a teen-ager, she walked five miles to a one-room school in south Alabama—and watched white children riding by in a bus. This was more than two decades ago, but Mrs. King, recalling her childhood in Perry County, Ala., said in an interview several years ago, "As far back as I can remember, I've been determined to do something to improve the situation."

Mrs. King's older sister, Edythe Bagley, 43, is a

school teacher in West Chester, Pa., who preceded Coretta at Antioch College in Yellow Springs, Ohio.

Their brother, Obie L. Scott Jr., 38, is a Methodist preacher for two small churches near Marion, Ala. He still lives with his parents at their rural home there.

He recalls that as a child Coretta was "very aggressive. She always tried to excell [sic] in everything she did," he said. "And she made good marks."

She had a temper, too, Scott said. And she used to fight. Coretta also picked cotton to help the family income during the Depression. She won a scholarship to Antioch, and worked as a waitress to earn her way.

Her father runs a country store and has for 20 years or more.

Intent on a singing career, she went from Antioch to Boston to study voice at the New England Conservatory of Music. There she met the young Baptist minister who was studying for his Ph.D. at Boston University.

Mrs. King recalled, "I wasn't interested in meeting a young minister at that time." Eighteen months later, on June 18, 1953, they were married in the garden of her parents' home.

The strong will that lies beneath the placid calm and dignity of her character was shown long before her husband was killed. She even tried to call President John F. Kennedy because her husband was in jail and she had not heard from him.

In 1963, when King was jailed in Birmingham, Ala., for leading a march, he was held incommunicado.

His worried wife tried to telephone President Kennedy "because I thought it was about the only thing I could do. I had not heard from my husband since his arrest."

Later, the president himself called Mrs. King and told her arrangements had been made for a phone call from her husband.

She marched beside him from Selma into Montgomery in 1965 in the triumphal climax to his drive for voting rights law. And she has sung in many concerts—and narrated civil rights history—to gain money for the cause.

In the early days of King's crusade as leader of a Negro boycott of buses in Montgomery, Mrs. King and 9-week-old Yolanda were at home when a bomb was thrown on the front porch and detonated with a shattering force. No one was hurt.

Neither the bomb nor other threats have deterred her from going wherever she could to raise an eloquent voice in the cause for her husband.

The high moment of her life came when he received the Nobel Peace prize. "I wish," she said then, "we could remain on this mountaintop forever."

The King home, still under a small security guard, is a simple one. Transparent seat covers are on the comfortable living room furniture.

The house is filled with mementoes. A portrait of Mahatma Gandhi given the Kings by the Gandhi Peace Foundation, hangs in the living room.

In the long green walled hallway leading to Mrs. King's bedroom, the only decoration is a portrait of King. Her bedroom is filled with pictures of her husband and children.

She is concerned now about the memorial most fitting for him.

"Bricks and stone and mortar would not be the kind of memorial he wanted," she has said. "He would have had slums cleared in his honor."

"WE HAVE A NATIONAL EMERGENCY," HE SAID. "FAILURE TO ACT WILL ONLY STRENGTHEN THE VOICES OF VIOLENCE AND GUERILLA WARFARE."

BUT HE SAID HE FELT RIOTS WOULD NOT INTENSIFY "IF AN ACT OF MASSIVE FAITH" WERE SHOWN BY CONGRESS. "IF NOT, WE WILL HAVE WORSE RIOTS THAN LAST YEAR."

HE SAID THE FIRST WAVES OF POOR WILL ARRIVE IN WASHINGTON APRIL 22. KING SAID THESE GROUPS WOULD "TAKE THE FORM OF LOBBYING IN CONGRESS" AND CALLED THEM "EDUCATIONAL DEMONSTRATORS."

HE SAID POOR PERSONS WOULD TRAVEL TO THE CAPITAL BY VARIOUS MEANS--WALKING, MULE TRAIN, HORSES AND BUGGIES. HE SAID THE FIRST GROUP WOULD LEAVE MISSISSIPPI, AND GO THROUGH ALABAMA, GEORGIA, SOUTH AND NORTH CAROLINA, PICKING UP OTHERS ON THEIR WAY.

(MORE)

KING NL

March 4, 1968

ATLANTA, Ga. (AP) – Dr. Martin Luther King Jr. said Monday he will meet soon with civil rights leaders who are "prone to violence" in an effort to make certain there are no riots during his poor people's campaign in Washington.

"I have no fear about riots at all," King declared at a news conference, in which he expanded on plans for the demonstrations and commented on the report of the president's commission on civil disorders.

King, who hopes to prevail on Congress to pass legislation providing jobs and income for the nation's poor, has called on thousands to march on the nation's capital. He said the march will begin April 22, the day Congress reconvenes after its Easter recess.

The civil rights leader said he will leave soon to visit various cities across the nation, meeting with civil rights leaders "who are prone to violence" in an effort at least "to neutralize them."

King said he had already met with Stokely Carmichael and Rap Brown, both militant black leaders. Both have given support to his campaign, he said.

"Carmichael has not agreed to participate but he has agreed to support us in principle," King said.

And he said the United Front, a coalition of militant black groups, has agreed to support the Washington march, sponsored by the Southern Christian Leadership Conference.

King praised the report of the president's national advisory commission on civil disorders and said "it reveals the absolute necessity of our spring campaign."

"The commission's report is a physician's warning of approaching death with a prescription to life. The duty of every American is to administer the remedy without cause for the cost and without delay," King said.

He said the commission is proposing reforms which have been recommended, sometimes in stronger fashion, by numerous other studies.

"Yet, nothing has been done," he declared. "This is why the Southern Christian Leadership Conference will lead masses of people to Washington in aggressive nonviolent demonstrations. The government must be confronted with the urgent need for reforms to fight poverty and racism."

"We have a national emergency," he said. "Failure to act will only strengthen the voices of violence and guerilla warfare."

But he said he felt riots would not intensify "if an act of massive faith" were shown by Congress. "If not, we will have worse riots than last year."

He said the first waves of poor will arrive in Washington April 22. King said these groups would "take the form of lobbying in Congress" and called them "educational demonstrators."

He said poor persons would travel to the capital by various means—walking, mule train, horses and buggies. He said the first group would leave Mississippi, and go through Alabama, Georgia, South and North Carolina, picking up others on their way.

"Our experience is that the federal government, and most especially Congress, never moves meaningfully against social ills until they are confronted directly and massively," King said.

He said other supporters of the march are the National Council of Churches and the American Friends Service Committee, a Quaker group. He said he has talked to more than 100 organizations who have promised support of the Washington demonstrations.

In 1963 not a single black was registered in some Mississippi counties composed of 80 per cent blacks. Of 450,000 blacks in that state of voting age, only 24,000 were registered. Ten years later, more than 280,000 blacks are registered.

In the spring of 1965, a significant and subtle change took place in the Negro's struggle upward. It happened in the cotton town of Selma, Ala., and came to a climax at the state Capitol in Montgomery.

King's target was discrimination against blacks at the ballot box. His method was a demonstration march, not a boycott as in the past, but a journey on foot for 50 miles from Selma to Montgomery.

DREAM ANNIVERSARY

Aug. 27, 1973

ATLANTA, Ga. AP – Ten years ago, 200,000 Americans gathered at the Lincoln Memorial and heard Dr. Martin Luther King Jr.'s stirring "I Have a Dream" speech, a high point of the movement which brought revolutionary gains to black America.

Even as King spoke of the "manacles of segregation and the chains of discrimination," his wife Coretta and other Southern blacks worried about how they would get home from Washington. In 1963, they were barred from many public accommodations.

But progress was on the way.

More than 100 congressmen heard King say in his

Aug. 28, 1963 speech that he still had a vision "deeply rooted in the American dream," and a year later, a sweeping civil rights bill was passed.

In politics, the Voting Rights Act of 1965 enfranchised two million new black voters and helped elect hundreds of Southern blacks to public offices, from city commissioners to congressmen.

In 1963 there were only about 200 elected black officials. Today there are nearly 3,000—1,152 of them from the South.

Mississippi has more elected black officials than any state in the nation and Alabama, the scene of crucial civil rights marches, is second.

Congress has three new black members, Yvonne Burke of Los Angeles, Barbara Jordan of Texas and the Rev. Andrew Young, who was a top aide of King's. Every Southern state has a[t] least one black state legislator, and Georgia has 16.

A substantial number of blacks have moved out of desperate poverty and expanding economic opportunities have nourished the development of a large, growing and increasingly visible black middle class.

John Lewis, who was brutally beaten in Alabama during the civil rights campaigns of the 1960s, says King's speech gave blacks "a sense of somebodyness. The Black movement changed the psyche of some people, particularly in the South."

Mrs. King says the single fact that blacks from all

over America and “especially those of us from the South” had to worry about how they would get home from Washington that day in ’63 “indicates the real changes that have occurred since.”

Despite the progress, however, the dream King spoke of still remains to be fully realized, his followers say.

Only five years ago, a presidential commission warned that without swift and decisive action, the United States would split into two societies, black and white, separate and unequal.

Blacks remain disproportionately poor. Nearly a third of this nation’s 23 million blacks live in poverty, and the economic gap between whites is widening, according to a recent Bureau of Census report.

A government commission recently characterized federal civil rights enforcement efforts as highly inadequate and said “large-scale discrimination continues.”

Jesse Jackson, who also marched with King, says:

“The main difference between ’63 and ’73 is that in ’63 we were fighting for citizenship: the right to vote, the right to go to school, the right to live in the neighborhood of our choice.

“But every item we’re fighting for now is a cost item. It costs to go to the school of your choice. It costs to live in the neighborhood of your choice. I think it is fitting that in 10 years the movement has gone from fighting for the right of survival to fighting for the means of survival."

Jackson, head of the fledgling Chicago-based organization PUSH—People United to Save Humanity—said he was impressed by the contrast recently when he attended an organization meeting in Alabama.

"When I got there, a black sheriff met me at the airport at Tuskegee. That's progress. I was allowed to sit anywhere I chose at the airport. That's progress. Most of the people I spoke to were registered voters. That's progress."

Jackson added, "There's one last mountain to conquer. That is the economic mountain."

For those millions of blacks still in dire poverty, Mrs. King says their conditions have in many ways worsened.

"They have been virtually cast aside by America," she said. "The 10 years since 1963 have only made their sweltering slums even more squalid. The range of social problems that grow from poverty when they are neglected have merely festered and worsened. For this sector of Black America, talk of progress is a cruel joke."

Young, who was the first black to be elected to Congress from Georgia in this century, says the 1970s have brought in a new era.

"It's clearer now than before that changes that will help the black man are the changes that will save the nation," said Young.

"If you save the cities, you're going to help blacks. If you're going to help blacks, you're going to help cities."

King said in his speech:

"I have a dream that one day even the State of Mississippi, a desert state sweltering with the heat of injustice and oppression, will be transformed into an oasis of freedom and justice..."

Two month earlier in Jackson, Miss., an NAACP field director, Medgar Evers, had been shot in the carport of his home.

Charles Evers, Medgar's brother, now mayor of Fayette, Miss., says, "White folks ain't quite as mean as they used to be," and predicts that "Mississippi is going ahead."

James H. Meredith, whose enrollment at the University of Mississippi precipitated riots, later moved back to his home state from New York, saying it was a better place to live.

Aaron Henry, one of the original members of the Mississippi Democratic Freedom party, says he thinks the advent of antipoverty program is one of the most significant changes in 10 years.

"In order to get an antipoverty program in your area you must have a biracial committee, 50-50. As a result, blacks have learned in Mississippi that all whites are not bad and whites have learned that all blacks are not bad," said Henry.

In 1963 not a single black was registered in some

Mississippi counties composed of 80 per cent blacks. Of 450,000 blacks in that state of voting age, only 24,000 were registered.

Ten years later, more than 280,000 blacks are registered.

In the spring of 1965, a significant and subtle change took place in the Negro's struggle upward. It happened in the cotton town of Selma, Ala., and came to a climax at the state Capitol in Montgomery.

King's target was discrimination against blacks at the ballot box. His method was a demonstration march, not a boycott as in the past, but a journey on foot for 50 miles from Selma to Montgomery.

A protest march unmatched in the history of the Negro revolution took place. Tens of thousands of blacks and whites took part.

Only 325 out of a potential 15,000 black voters were registered in Dallas County, which includes Selma. Of the county's total population of 55,000 slightly more than 57 per cent were blacks.

In Dallas County today, more than 67 per cent of blacks are registered. Blacks now control Greene County, Ala., and in nearby Lowndes County, which was nearly 80 per cent black in 1963 with not a single black registered voter, more than 60 per cent of the blacks are registered.

Since King's speech, many feel the civil rights movement has become divided and weakened. The Southern

Christian Leadership Conference, which King founded, has waned in influence and national prominence since his death in 1968.

"If my husband were alive today," said Coretta King, "he would look at the achievements of the years since 1963 with pride, and he would find the basis for renewed optimism.

"But he would face the years ahead with the same splendid moral outrage at the continuing stain of injustice, and the same fierce determination to end it forever, that moved America when they heard him speak on that day 10 years ago."

ACKNOWLEDGMENTS

The Associated Press would like to thank the following for their contributions to this project: Andrew Young; Tom Curley; Tom Jory; Chris Sullivan; Valerie Komor; Francesca Pitaro; Sarit Hand; Paul Colford; Ellen Hale; Aashka Dave; the staff at RosettaBooks; and of course, Kathryn Johnson.